BRIDGE FOR
AMBITIOUS PLAYERS

Terence Reese

LONDON
VICTOR GOLLANCZ
in association with
PETER CRAWLEY

First published in Great Britain March 1988
in association with Peter Crawley
by Victor Gollancz Ltd
Fourth impression March 1994
in association with Peter Crawley
by Victor Gollancz
A Cassell imprint
Villiers House, 41/47 Strand, London WC2N 5JE

A catalogue record for this book
is available from the British Library

ISBN 0-575-04176-5

Printed in Great Britain by
St Edmundsbury Press Ltd, Bury St Edmunds, Suffolk

BRIDGE FOR AMBITIOUS PLAYERS

A new book by Terence Reese is always a welcome event. The author is a European and World Champion, and was for many years an automatic choice for the British team. His name is synonymous with good bridge writing.

Here the maestro directs his attention towards those players who are already half-way up the ladder and shows them how to climb the remaining rungs that stand between them and success. Each of the sixty-five deals contains at least one instructional point not normally found in a textbook. The player with ambition who studies these hands will surely notice a marked improvement in his game.

The bonus, as we have come to expect from this author, is that the lucid style and laconic wit make for a highly enjoyable read.

'Terence Reese is at his commanding best in *Bridge for Ambitious Players*, bringing to life an excellent selection of hands in his admirably economic style.'
— Jeremy Flint, *The Times*

by Terence Reese in the *Master Bridge Series*

Do You Really Want to Win At Bridge?
(based on the French text by Pierre Béguin & Jean Besse)

with Roger Trézel
Blocking and Unblocking Plays in Bridge
Safety Plays in Bridge · Elimination Plays in Bridge
Snares and Swindles in Bridge
Those Extra Chances in Bridge
When to Duck, When to Win in Bridge
The Art of Defence in Bridge
The Mistakes You Make at Bridge

with Jeremy Flint
Bridge with the Professional Touch

with José le Dentu
Bridge: Triumphs and Disasters

with Rixi Markus
Better Bridge for Club Players

with David Bird
Miracles of Card Play · Unholy Tricks
Doubled and Venerable · Cardinal Sins
Bridge – Tricks of the Trade
All You Need to Know About Bidding
All You Need to Know About Play

with Julian Pottage
Positive Defence · Positive Declarer's Play
The Extra Edge in Play

Contents

Foreword

In Britain, and no doubt in many other countries, there are perhaps a hundred players of international standard and upwards of a thousand who have ability and experience but know they are not quite in the top class. This book is designed for players in that range and for others who are not far behind. It is, fortunately, easier to move up in bridge than in most games. Most players simply do not make the effort.

The book is divided into four parts, but the distinctions are somewhat arbitrary and not important. You may read straight through or 'dip in'. You will be glad of one thing: the examples are all on facing pages.

Part 1 – Mainly Play

Deals 1– 20

1

Too True

It is fairly easy to play against opponents who always false-card in certain situations and also easy to play against opponents who seldom false-card. On the following deal South was able to form a certain conclusion about the lie of the hearts.

Dealer South   Game all

	♠ K J 10 4	
	♡ K 7 5	
	◇ Q	
	♣ A K 9 6 2	

♠ 6 3		♠ 8
♡ 10 8 6 2	N W E S	♡ A Q J 9 3
◇ J 10 8 7		◇ 9 5 4 3 2
♣ J 7 5		♣ Q 10

	♠ A Q 9 7 5 2	
	♡ 4	
	◇ A K 6	
	♣ 8 4 3	

It was easy to reach six spades:

South	West	North	East
1♠	No	3♣	No
3♠	No	4NT	No
5♡	No	6♠	No
No	No		

South won the diamond lead in dummy, drew trumps, and played a third round to see if anything would happen. Immediately East completed a heavy peter in hearts, dropping the queen and then the 3.

As East was the sort of player who could be believed, South abandoned the natural play of leading a heart towards the king. Instead, he discarded two hearts on the top diamonds and played for this ending:

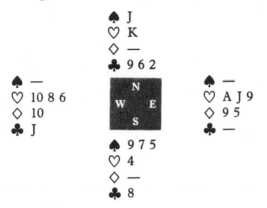

♠ J
♡ K
◇ —
♣ 9 6 2

♠ —
♡ 10 8 6
◇ 10
♣ J

♠ —
♡ A J 9
◇ 9 5
♣ —

♠ 9 7 5
♡ 4
◇ —
♣ 8

Now the king of hearts left East with the lead and the reflection that there is no percentage in being a George Washington at the bridge table.

Note that South's line would also have succeeded if West, after all, had held the ace of hearts and only two clubs.

2

Five Plus One

'That's typical of my luck at this game,' said South after putting a 3NT contract on the floor. 'Queen of hearts, queen of spades, king of clubs all in the wrong hand, the hearts didn't break and the diamonds didn't break. That makes five things wrong on one hand.'

'There was one other,' said North solemnly.

'Oh, what was that?' asked South, rushing in.

'The way you played it.'

Dealer South   Game all

	♠ A J 4	
	♡ J 6 2	
	◇ K Q 5 3	
	♣ Q 9 4	

♠ 7 3		♠ Q 10 8 6 2
♡ 10 9 4 3	N W E S	♡ Q 7
◇ J 9 7 2		◇ 10
♣ 10 7 5		♣ K J 8 6 3

	♠ K 9 5	
	♡ A K 8 5	
	◇ A 8 6 4	
	♣ A 2	

There was no problem in the bidding:

South	West	North	East
1NT	No	3NT	No
No	No		

I think I would have begun with a heart on the West hand, preferring the major suit to the minor, but West chose a low diamond, which ran to the 10 and ace. Holding eight tricks on top,

South tried a low heart to the jack. On this occasion the play of the ace and king would have turned out better, but South's method was not far wrong, as it would have gained against four to the queen in the West hand.

East headed the jack of hearts with the queen and returned a heart. South played a second round of diamonds, then a third round of hearts, followed by a spade finesse. East won again and returned a spade. A club to the queen and king proved equally disappointing and in time South lost a trick to West in each red suit.

Obviously the contract can be made in several ways, but apart from 'wrong views' South made two definite, identifiable errors. What were they?

First, it would have been better to play one top heart and a low heart, rather than an immediate low heart to the jack. When East wins with the queen he has no good return.

Secondly, and less obvious, was it necessary to capture the 10 of diamonds at trick one? If West has led fourth best, which is the natural assumption, any return by East will inevitably present declarer with a ninth trick.

3

Doubting Thomasina

'Do good players really foresee the clever end-games we read about in your articles?' asked a doubting Thomasina from Cornwall.

I sympathize with the sceptical point of view because, being a moderate chess player myself, I wonder sometimes about the inner truth of those annotations by the masters which begin, 'Not so-and-so because of such-and-such', the perils of such-and-such being analysed over fourteen moves.

No doubt the master chess player has a feel for tricky situations, which makes it unnecessary for him to analyse in detail. At bridge it is not, after all, necessary to analyse very far, because the same situations constantly occur. It is not difficult, once one has the knack, to foresee a standard situation that will arise six or seven tricks later. This applies especially to elimination play, where it is often not necessary to form a picture of the opposing hands. Take a simple deal like this one:

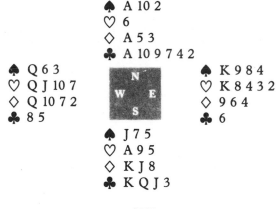

```
                    ♠ A 10 2
                    ♡ 6
                    ♢ A 5 3
                    ♣ A 10 9 7 4 2
♠ Q 6 3                              ♠ K 9 8 4
♡ Q J 10 7          N               ♡ K 8 4 3 2
♢ Q 10 7 2        W   E             ♢ 9 6 4
♣ 8 5               S               ♣ 6
                    ♠ J 7 5
                    ♡ A 9 5
                    ♢ K J 8
                    ♣ K Q J 3
```

At rubber bridge the North-South hands were bid in a sensible style that would seldom be matched in the tournament world.

South	West	North	East
1♣	No	2◇	No
2NT	No	4♣	No
4◇	No	5♣	No
No	No		

West led the queen of hearts and when he won with the ace of hearts South claimed the contract with a speed which you may think immodest. The jargon runs: 'Eliminate hearts (i.e. ruff out all the hearts held by South), draw trumps, play off ◇ A K and exit with the third diamond.'

This leads to the classic situation where the defenders must either open up the spades or concede a ruff-and-discard. Say that West wins the third diamond and leads a spade to his partner's king: now East will be 'on play', forced either to return a spade into the tenace or a heart, allowing South to ruff in one hand while discarding from the other.

4

Back to Life

'I suppose you get most of your hands from readers,' a friend said to me recently. Not many as a matter of fact; but this one had two interesting points:

Dealer South   Love all

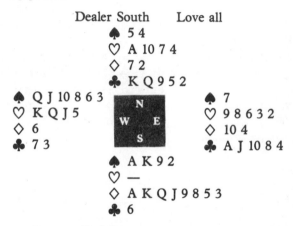

```
                  ♠ 5 4
                  ♡ A 10 7 4
                  ◇ 7 2
                  ♣ K Q 9 5 2
♠ Q J 10 8 6 3                    ♠ 7
♡ K Q J 5          N              ♡ 9 8 6 3 2
◇ 6            W       E          ◇ 10 4
♣ 7 3              S              ♣ A J 10 8 4
                  ♠ A K 9 2
                  ♡ —
                  ◇ A K Q J 9 8 5 3
                  ♣ 6
```

'Your readers may find this deal amusing,' wrote a correspondent from the midlands. 'We were pleased because we noticed an unusual type of defence. The bidding went:

South	West	North	East
2◇	2♠	3♣	Dble
6◇	No	No	No

'Not very scientific, but the final contract was reasonable. West led the king of hearts and the declarer won in dummy, discarding his singleton club. He led the king of clubs from the table and ruffed East's ace. Then he led off ace and king of spades. East ruffed the second round and returned a heart.

'Now the two outstanding trumps fell together. Declarer was able to ruff one spade and discard the other on the queen of clubs.

'Amateurs though we are, we noted that East could have defeated the contract by refusing to ruff the second spade. I argued that a good player would have seen this in time, but the others didn't agree. What do you think?'

Well, let's say that a good player would be annoyed with himself if he *didn't* see it.

There is another good point in the deal. Declarer has a better line of play. Remembering that West has bid spades, he should play low from dummy on the opening heart lead, draw trumps, and cash two spades. Then he leads a club and East, having no spades, must bring the dummy back to life by exiting with a heart or a club. One spade goes away on the ace of hearts and one on the queen of clubs. (East doubled three clubs, remember, so he surely holds the ace.)

5

Marooned

'I counted up to nine', said South pathetically, after failing in 3NT on the deal below. Perhaps he did count, but while arithmetic is useful at bridge, it isn't everything.

Deal North   Love all

♠ A K 3
♡ K
◇ 9 8 6 5 2
♣ 9 7 4 3

♠ J 8 2
♡ Q 9 3
◇ Q J 4
♣ Q 10 6 5

♠ Q 9 5
♡ J 7 6 4 2
◇ 10 7
♣ K J 2

♠ 10 7 6 4
♡ A 10 8 5
◇ A K 3
♣ A 8

The bidding went:

South	West	North	East
1♡	No	2◇(1)	No
2NT(2)	No	3NT	No
No	No		

(1) I find it quite easy to respond 1NT rather than two diamonds on a hand like this. Ten points there may be, but the high cards are not well situated.

(2) Showing 15–17 in old-fashioned Acol.

When West led ♣5 and East played the king, South won at once with the ace. This was correct, because it would block the suit if West held five clubs and East K J or K 10 alone. South began with ace, king and another diamond. West took his club tricks and South finished one down, because he was unable to reach his hand to cash the ace of hearts. He lost a diamond, three clubs and a spade.

'I suppose I ought to have cashed the king of hearts earlier', said the declarer.

'That doesn't help,' North replied. 'It is still dangerous to cash the ace of hearts before losing a diamond trick. But I think you should have begun with ace of diamonds and a low diamond.'

This is not quite good enough, either; West can exit with a third diamond and again the ace of hearts is marooned.

It is all right to lead a heart to the king and then play ace of diamonds and a low one. Alternatively, South can begin with a low diamond from hand, retaining both high cards.

It's not easy to frame any general advice about these hands where a singleton honour (the king of hearts) is capable of causing a block. Just recognize that there may be a problem and don't lay down a card until you are fairly sure you can make your tricks separately.

6

Make the Pieces Fit

One of the mysteries of the game is that the type of thinking known as 'second-degree assumption' is seldom put into practice at the table. Yet it cannot be rare. It occurs in this type of situation:

West	*East*
♠ K J	♠ x x
♡ x x	♡ A Q
◇ —	◇ —
♣ —	♣ —

Imagine that West needs to make at least two tricks from this combination of cards. He leads a spade from dummy and has to decide whether to play the jack or the king. Assume, also, that South has already turned up with some top cards. It is sensible now to think on these lines: 'If the heart finesse is right, no worry, so I will assume it is wrong. In that case the odds will be against South holding the ace of spades as well; thus it must be right to finesse the spade jack.'

Assume, next, that declarer needs three tricks from these cards. He must assume now that the heart finesse is right. It then becomes (or may become) more likely that South will hold the ace of spades, so now the odds will favour the play of the spade king.

Thinking on these lines will sometimes point to a play that in a mathematical sense is against the odds.

West	*East*
♠ K 9 7 6 5 4	♠ J 8 3 2
♡ 6	♡ A 5 4 2
◇ A Q 10 7	◇ J 9 8
♣ K 6	♣ 10 7

North–South are playing weak two bids and the bidding goes:

South	West	North	East
2♡	2♠	3♣	3♠
No	4♠	No	No
No			

North leads the queen of hearts, the ace wins and South plays the jack. A low spade is led from dummy and South plays the 10. Should West play low or go up with the king, and why? This is how West should reason:

(1) No doubt North (who bid three clubs) holds the ace of clubs. That gives me three top losers – a spade and two clubs.

(2) To have any chance of making the contract, therefore, I must assume that the diamond king is held by South.

(3) South can hardly hold a fair suit of hearts, king of diamonds and ace of spades as well. I must play North for a singleton ace of spades.

And that's how it was. South held ♠ Q 10   ♡ K J 10 9 7 3 ◇ K 5   ♣ 4 3 2.

7

Unrecorded Crime

At the end of a long championship match there is often some pundit who will prepare what is called a 'crime sheet', supposedly indicating the cost of the mistakes that various players have made. This always seems to me a most unsatisfactory way of determining who played well and who did not. So much takes place at the game which does not appear on the scoresheet (and screens make very little difference). I am thinking of a hand such as the following:

Dealer South   E–W vulnerable

```
                  ♠ A K Q 7 5 2
                  ♡ A J 3 2
                  ◇ 10 6 3
                  ♣ —
  ♠ J 9 4                        ♠ 10
  ♡ 8 6            N             ♡ 10 9 7
  ◇ A Q 7 2     W     E          ◇ 5 4
  ♣ A Q 8 4        S             ♣ 10 9 7 6 5 3 2
                  ♠ 8 6 3
                  ♡ K Q 5 4
                  ◇ K J 9 8
                  ♣ K J
```

This was the recorded bidding:

South	West	North	East
1♡	No	2♠	No
2NT	No	3♡	No
3NT	No	4♣	No
4◇	No	6♡	No
No	No		

West, who had shown a good deal of interest as the auction progressed, led a trump. There may seem to be twelve tricks, with the hearts breaking 3–2, but this is not so, because for entry reasons South cannot ruff two clubs and return to draw trumps. It looks as though he will have to finesse in diamonds, but instead he drew trumps and cashed the spades, to arrive at this ending:

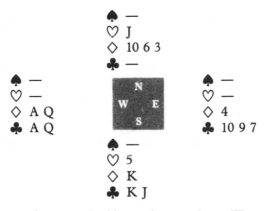

A diamond went to the king and ace, and now West was on play, the victim of his own pregnant pauses and foolish questions.

8

A Special Art

In one of my books – I think it was *Reese on Play* – I remarked that squeeze play was different from all other skills in the game. What I meant was that some good players had little understanding of this subject, while some quite moderate players had a fair grasp. If you study South's problem on the following deal you will be able to form an opinion about your own standing.

Dealer South   Love all

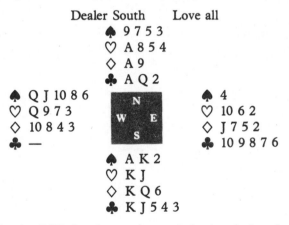

Playing in 6NT, South won the spade lead and played a club to the ace, on which West showed out. A finesse of ♡ J failed, and now the entry situation was unfavourable for any squeeze. (The difficulty lies in the heart block.)

After the first round of clubs South should have ducked a spade to rectify the count, as it is called. He plays for this ending:

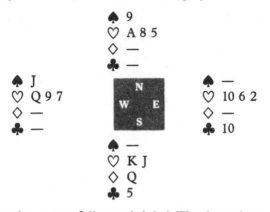

♠ 9
♥ A 8 5
♦ —
♣ —

♠ J
♥ Q 9 7
♦ —
♣ —

♠ —
♥ 10 6 2
♦ —
♣ 10

♠ —
♥ K J
♦ Q
♣ 5

When the queen of diamonds is led, West has to keep a spade and East a club, so neither can keep a guard in hearts. The jack of hearts, presenting the chance for a finesse, was an illusion.

If you find this hand puzzling in any respect, then it will be well worth your while to study the principles of squeeze play at some length.*

* For example, in *Simple Squeezes*, by Hugh Kelsey (Gollancz).

9

Chance for Early Claim

When the declarer in a slam contract sees that he has just eleven tricks on top, with no finesse positions, it is usually good play to give up a trick early on, in preparation for a squeeze. But in the meantime it is important not to give the defenders a chance to destroy any of the cards that threaten them. South failed to find the right solution on the following hand:

Dealer East   N–S vulnerable

```
                    ♠ 8 6 5 2
                    ♡ 6 5 4
                    ◇ A K 6
                    ♣ Q 3 2
    ♠ J 4                            ♠ —
    ♡ —                              ♡ Q J 10 9 8 7 3
    ◇ Q 9 8 5          N             ◇ J 10 2
    ♣ A K 10 9 7 5 4  W   E          ♣ J 8 6
                        S
                    ♠ A K Q 10 9 7 3
                    ♡ A K 2
                    ◇ 7 4 3
                    ♣ —
```

East opened with a pre-emptive three hearts and the bidding continued:

South	West	North	East
—	—	—	3♡
4♠	No	5◇	No
6♠	No	No	No

North would not have fought against his partner's four spades with a minor suit, so his five diamonds could be interpreted as a slam try in spades.

West led the king of clubs. South ruffed, drew trumps, and looked around. Too late! The only chance now for a squeeze was to duck a heart and then find West with five diamonds and the ace of clubs. This plan failed because East was able to keep three diamonds.

The hand plays very simply if South, instead of ruffing the club lead, discards a diamond. Then a squeeze is certain to succeed, because West will be obliged to keep the ace of clubs and East at least three hearts. It will be impossible for either of them to guard the diamonds. In fact, South may claim the contract without playing another card – always assuming that the defenders will trust him to know when the two of hearts has become a winner.

If South, after ruffing the first club, attempts to restore the count by ducking the next club, the defence must of course kill the club menace by leading a third round. From then on, West can guard the diamonds and East the hearts.

10

All Under Control

Some plays in bridge are admittedly baffling – so much so that even with all the cards exposed the winning line is not easy to see. Suppose you arrive at six hearts on this deal and a trump is led. How would you set about it?

Dealer South   Game all

```
                 ♠ 5
                 ♡ K 6 4
                 ◇ K Q 7 4 3
                 ♣ A K 6 2
 ♠ Q 10 8 4          N          ♠ K J 7
 ♡ 9 8 7 5        W     E       ♡ 10 2
 ◇ 10 5             S           ◇ J 9 8 2
 ♣ Q 10 8                       ♣ J 9 7 5
                 ♠ A 9 6 3 2
                 ♡ A Q J 3
                 ◇ A 6
                 ♣ 4 3
```

The bidding might go:

South	West	North	East
1♠	No	2◇	No
2♡	No	3♣	No
3◇	No	4♡	No
6♡	No	No	No

West leads the nine of hearts. It is easy to count twelve tricks, but not so easy to make them. With both red suits breaking 4-2 you can count four tricks in hearts, four in diamonds, ace of spades and a spade ruff, two top clubs. But what is the precise sequence of play? Suppose you go up with the king of hearts, take one spade ruff, then draw trumps. The problem now is that you will be exposed to the wind when you give up a diamond trick.

The solution on this type of hand is to give up the trick in the side suit while everything is under control. Win with the king of hearts, then duck a diamond at trick two! Win the trump return, take a spade ruff, and then the position will be:

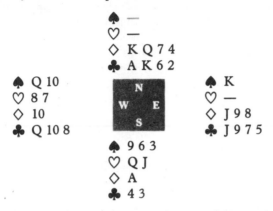

```
              ♠ —
              ♡ —
              ◇ K Q 7 4
              ♣ A K 6 2
  ♠ Q 10                      ♠ K
  ♡ 8 7          N            ♡ —
  ◇ 10       W     E          ◇ J 9 8
  ♣ Q 10 8       S            ♣ J 9 7 5
              ♠ 9 6 3
              ♡ Q J
              ◇ A
              ♣ 4 3
```

No problem now; you cross to the ace of diamonds, draw the trumps, and claim the remainder.

11

Ely Said It First

The old-fashioned forcing response, such as two hearts over one
diamond, has become – well, it has become old-fashioned. In
America, particularly, a jump response tends to show either a very
rare giant or, for some players, a long suit in a weak hand. It may be
right not to force when you have no fit, but when you have a good
suit of your own, or strong support for partner, it must be sensible
to make a jump response. As Culbertson pointed out more than 50
years ago, you don't save time by making a minimum response,
because you have to jump later; or bid around the clock, giving no
picture of what you hold.

In a pairs event several North–South players failed to reach a
slam on this hand:

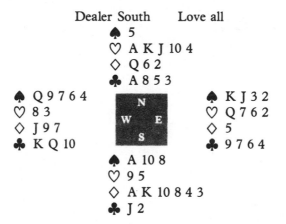

Dealer South   Love all

When South opened one diamond and North responded one
heart, the partnership tended to miss the slam. Mind you, it was just

as well, because most of them failed to make twelve tricks.

Say that West leads the king of clubs against six diamonds. South should win, cash just one high diamond, then play ace and king of hearts. This leaves:

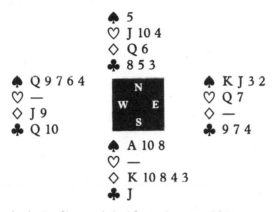

```
              ♠ 5
              ♡ J 10 4
              ◇ Q 6
              ♣ 8 5 3
♠ Q 9 7 6 4        N        ♠ K J 3 2
♡ —           W       E     ♡ Q 7
◇ J 9             S         ◇ —
♣ Q 10                      ♣ 9 7 4
              ♠ A 10 8
              ♡ —
              ◇ K 10 8 4 3
              ♣ J
```

Now the jack of hearts is led from dummy. If East covers with the queen, South ruffs high, returns to the queen of diamonds, and discards ♣ J on ♡ 10. If East plays low on the jack of hearts, South simply discards his club loser. You will find that other lines of play are quite likely to fail.

12

Trick to Spare

'How did it go?' I asked Rixi Markus on one occasion after the third session of the pairs at Juan-Les-Pins.

'Badly; my partner (it was Louis Tarlo) went down in a lay-down 6NT' was the uncompromising reply.

'I don't remember a slam for North–South in notrumps,' I said. 'Perhaps we didn't play it.'

'It was board 23,' she said, pointing it out on the mimeographed sheet which is handed to competitors after the session. 'You played it in 3NT, I expect.'

This was the hand:

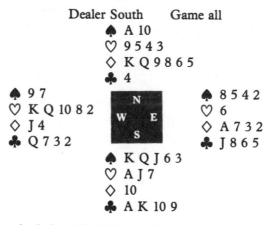

Dealer South   Game all

                ♠ A 10
                ♡ 9 5 4 3
                ◇ K Q 9 8 6 5
                ♣ 4

♠ 9 7   ♠ 8 5 4 2
♡ K Q 10 8 2   ♡ 6
◇ J 4   ◇ A 7 3 2
♣ Q 7 3 2   ♣ J 8 6 5

                ♠ K Q J 6 3
                ♡ A J 7
                ◇ 10
                ♣ A K 10 9

Yes, we had played in 3NT, making five. It hadn't struck me that we had missed a slam. However, at the table under discussion the bidding had been:

South	North
Tarlo	Markus
1♠	2♦
3NT	6NT
No	

'We had been doing badly, I had to bring in some points,' Rixi explained when I permitted myself a slight frown. 'The king of hearts was led and there were twelve tricks on top, but he went down.'

If you were playing anything from 3NT to 5NT, a possibility would be to drop the jack of hearts under the king, hoping that West would follow with a low one. But that wouldn't help in 6NT. Win with the ace of hearts, Rixi said, lead the 10 of diamonds and overtake. East will probably duck, so then you lead the king of diamonds and pin West's jack. Now you not only have twelve tricks, but one to spare!

Yes, I suppose that is the best line. Or might you win with ace of hearts and run the 10 of diamonds, picking up J x x in the West hand? No, East will hold off. You cross to ace of spades and force out the diamond ace, but now a club from East will be very inconvenient in terms of entries.

13

Not Popular

Counting a hand is the beginning, and not far from the end, of all good play. It is not a difficult process – you never need to go beyond the number 13 – but most players tend to be lazy in this department of the game.

Let's see how easy (or difficult) it was on this hand where my partner, South, was in five spades doubled.

Dealer West   E–W vulnerable

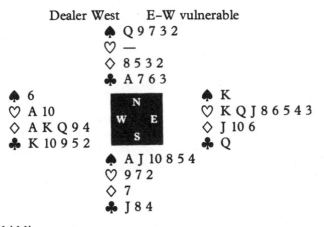

```
                    ♠ Q 9 7 3 2
                    ♡ —
                    ◇ 8 5 3 2
                    ♣ A 7 6 3
♠ 6                                      ♠ K
♡ A 10              N                    ♡ K Q J 8 6 5 4 3
◇ A K Q 9 4    W         E               ◇ J 10 6
♣ K 10 9 5 2        S                    ♣ Q
                    ♠ A J 10 8 5 4
                    ♡ 9 7 2
                    ◇ 7
                    ♣ J 8 4
```

The bidding went:

South	West	North	East
—	1◇	No	1♡
1♠	2♣	2♠	4♡
No	No	4♠	No
No	5♡	No	No
5♠	No	No	No

If East had responded four hearts on the first round he would doubtless have bought the contract.

In five spades doubled South ruffed the second diamond, drew a round of trumps, and cross-ruffed to arrive at this position:

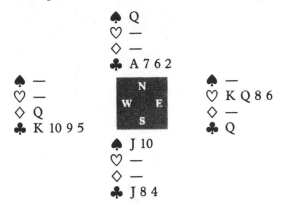

At this point my partner played ace and another club, losing two tricks to West. 'I hoped to find East with K 10 or Q 10,' he informed me.

'You might have done,' I replied. 'If East had started with fourteen cards, that is.'

It was the kind of remark that makes me unpopular, but you can see the point. Having assessed the distribution, South had to exit with a low club, playing East for a singleton queen, king or ten.

14

Look Left, Look Right

That engaging writer, S.J. Simon, used to give odd little pieces of advice, and one was never quite sure whether he meant them to be taken seriously or not. 'When you are dummy,' he wrote once, 'see which suit has been led and put it down last. Then the declarer must look at the whole hand before he can play a card.' I tried that system on the following deal, but it didn't help.

Dealer North   Game all

```
                    ♠ 6 5
                    ♡ A Q 4
                    ◇ K 6 3
                    ♣ A 10 8 7 5
  ♠ 7 3 2                          ♠ 8 4
  ♡ 10 7 3 2         N             ♡ K J 9 5
  ◇ Q 8 7 2      W       E         ◇ J 10 4
  ♣ 6 4              S             ♣ Q J 9 2
                    ♠ A K Q J 10 9
                    ♡ 8 6
                    ◇ A 9 5
                    ♣ K 3
```

My partner and I reached six spades with a speed that in these days would attract the attention of the traffic police:

South	North
—	1♣
2♠	2NT
6♠	No

West led a low heart and I followed Simon's prescription, putting the dummy down slowly, suit by suit, keeping the hearts to the end.

But as soon as he had seen A Q x South reached for the queen. East won and played well by returning the jack of hearts and forcing the ace. Now South was short of an entry to establish and cash dummy's fifth club.

The right line here was to play low from dummy at trick one. Then the heart entry cannot be dislodged and the fifth club will supply a discard for the diamond loser.

But you may say – and I won't dispute it – that it was mostly my fault. I could have transferred six spades to 6NT, played from the North side. The discards on the spades would have been difficult for the defenders, and one way or another I think I would have landed 6NT.

I am sometimes asked whether I knew Skid Simon (his Russian name was Skidelsky) and whether I ever played with him. Yes, indeed! I played one or two sessions with him both at Copenhagen (1948) and in Paris (1949). He was just as amusing off stage, as it were, as on. He was a fine player and would have been better still had he taken more care of his health. If he had to travel 200 yards it was 'Taxi!' (whether or not he had any money in his pocket to pay for it). I did a television show with him the night before he died, towards the end of 1949.

15

No Change

It seems odd now, but at one time in bridge history there was a great deal of argument about a situation of this kind:

A Q J 6 3

10 9

Suppose that, as the play develops in other suits, it becomes apparent that West began with five cards of this suit, East with only one. West discards three times and follows with a low card when you lead from 10 9 to dummy's A Q. At this stage you know that West has one card left and East has one card. Is it reasonable to suppose that now East's singleton is as likely to be the king as a low card?

Well, I won't go into long explanations, but the fact is that the initial odds are unchanged. If West began with five of the suit, and East with a singleton, it is five to one on West's last card being the king.

But of course there may be special considerations. I happened to be South on this deal from a match between England and Northern Ireland:

Dealer West   N–S vulnerable

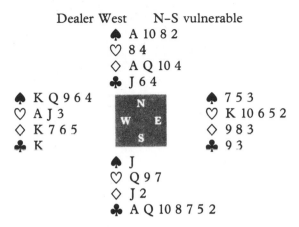

♠ A 10 8 2
♡ 8 4
♢ A Q 10 4
♣ J 6 4

♠ K Q 9 6 4
♡ A J 3
♢ K 7 6 5
♣ K

♠ 7 5 3
♡ K 10 6 5 2
♢ 9 8 3
♣ 9 3

♠ J
♡ Q 9 7
♢ J 2
♣ A Q 10 8 7 5 2

My partner and I bid somewhat aggressively after West had opened one spade:

South	West	North	East
—	1♠	No	No
2♣	No	2NT	No
3♣	No	4♣	No
5♣	No	No	No

Having won the spade lead in dummy, I led the jack of clubs and East played the nine. It occurred to me now that if West had held A K of hearts he would probably have led from this suit rather than the king of spades. If East held a high card in hearts he would not hold the king of clubs. Apart from which, the king of clubs is (as they say) always single.

A string of clubs then proved very embarrassing for West, and I ended with twelve tricks. 'Sorry, partner, I couldn't quite bid six!'

16

Own Goal

It is evidence of a bad character, I know, but for me a show-jumper parting company with his mount, an ice-skater landing with a bump, or a back pass trickling across the goal-line, are amusing occasions, made funnier by the horrified tones of the commentator. The same sort of thing can happen at bridge. This was a celebrated hand from a match between Scotland and Northern Ireland.

Dealer North   Game all

♠ Q 5 2
♡ K J 7 6
◇ J 10 7
♣ A Q 6

♠ 4 3
♡ Q 10 8 3
◇ 9 6 4 3
♣ 8 5 4

♠ J 8
♡ 9 5 4 2
◇ K 8 2
♣ J 10 7 2

♠ A K 10 9 7 6
♡ A
◇ A Q 5
♣ K 9 3

The Scottish North–South were Hugh Kelsey, author of many fine books on the game, and Tom Culbertson (no relation). They bid as follows:

South	West	North	East
—	—	1NT	No
3♠	No	4♣	No
5NT	No	6♣(1)	No
7♠(2)	No	No	No

(1) One top honour in the trump suit.
(2) The grand is likely to be on a finesse at worst.

Seven spades looks a lay-down with the diamond finesse right. However, South gave himself the chance of bringing down the queen of hearts in three rounds and reached this end position:

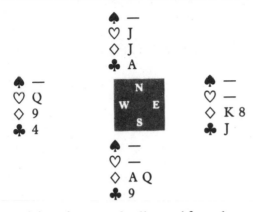

After a club to the ace and a diamond from dummy South has to work out whether the diamond finesse is right or whether West, starting with ♡ Q and ◇ K, has been forced to bare the diamond king. There was a slight clue pointing to the second possibility. West had led a club from 8 5 4. With 9 6 4 3 of diamonds he might equally have led a diamond. The principle of restricted choice suggests that West began with ◇ K and preferred a club for that reason. So Hugh Kelsey played for the drop and lost a big swing.

17

Double Chance

'What did you do on board 9?' a team-mate asked me when I rejoined her table.

'They played in 3NT and made seven', I answered. 'Sorry, I gave them a trick by holding up the king of diamonds. Did you bid the slam in diamonds? Well done, it wasn't easy.'

'No, we played in 3NT too. And I'm afraid I was one down.'

Dealer South   N–S vulnerable

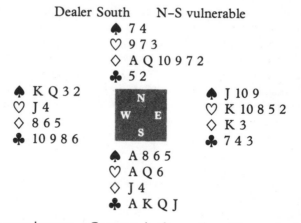

```
                    ♠ 7 4
                    ♡ 9 7 3
                    ◇ A Q 10 9 7 2
                    ♣ 5 2
♠ K Q 3 2                           ♠ J 10 9
♡ J 4              N                ♡ K 10 8 5 2
◇ 8 6 5         W     E             ◇ K 3
♣ 10 9 8 6         S                ♣ 7 4 3
                    ♠ A 8 6 5
                    ♡ A Q 6
                    ◇ J 4
                    ♣ A K Q J
```

The occasion was a Congress in the north and I was playing in a team with the organizer and his wife. At my table North–South had bid as follows:

South	West	North	East
1♣	No	1◇	No
3NT	No	No	No

It is not a particularly easy hand to bid to six diamonds, because North may well think that 6NT would be safer. He should perhaps bid four diamonds over 3NT and see where that leads.

My partner led the 10 of clubs in preference to a low spade. South won and led the jack of diamonds, overtaking with the queen. When I let this hold, he took the heart finesse – good play. When this won he could see nine tricks, so he took no more risk and dropped my king of diamonds, ending with thirteen tricks.

At the other table the lady organizer had opened 2NT, as players do when they can count their 21 points. The response on the North hand was a little awkward, because three diamonds would have been a transfer to hearts. He settled for 3NT, and there they rested.

Again, West led the ten of clubs. South led the jack of diamonds but did not think of overtaking, to test the heart position. When the jack held she finessed again – wrong because there was the double chance of dropping the king of diamonds or making nine tricks with the aid of the heart finesse.

18

Time to Reflect

Some players go into a meditative trance on almost every hand they play, presumably wondering how to overcome exceptionally bad breaks. Such players are exasperating when you are playing against them, but on the deal below my partner belonged to this type and I had reason to be grateful. He was not a strong player, really, but as a result of careful thought he made a contract on which many better players would have failed.

Dealer South   Love all

```
                    ♠ K 10 8
                    ♡ J 8 6 5
                    ◇ 8
                    ♣ A K J 5 4
    ♠ J 7 6 5 2                        ♠ Q 9 4 3
    ♡ A              N                  ♡ 4 3 2
    ◇ 6 4         W     E               ◇ 10 9 7 3 2
    ♣ Q 10 9 8 2     S                  ♣ 7
                    ♠ A
                    ♡ K Q 10 9 7
                    ◇ A K Q J 5
                    ♣ 6 3
```

South (my partner) opened with an Acol two-bid, though most players would have been content with a simple one heart. The bidding continued:

South	West	North	East
2♡	No	3♣	No
3◇	No	4♡(1)	No
4NT	No	5◇	No
6♡	No	No	No

(1) You may judge from this bid (I should have temporized with three hearts and advanced later) that I did not exactly trust him.

How wrong I was! West led a club to dummy's king. Most players, it must be said, would have led a trump at trick two and been defeated. My present partner, after his usual long consideration, came to hand with the ace of spades, played ace of diamonds and ruffed a diamond, then disposed of his dangerous club on the king of spades. This way, he was safe against any distribution.

Going back to the auction, I don't consider it a crime to open two hearts. If South opens one heart, the bidding might go:

South	North
1♡	2♣
2♢	4♡
4NT	5♢
6♡	No

South would not be wrong to jump on the second round, but since the change of suit, after a response at the two level, is normally played as forcing, two diamonds is sufficient. A jump at this point would imply a good fit for clubs.

19

Ready to Move

It is common for a declarer to set out with one plan and later abandon it for another when he finds that the original plan won't work, but sometimes it is not so easy to switch the line of attack. The deal below was played in the semi-final of the Gold Cup – and misplayed, though in a different degree, at both tables.

Dealer South   Game all

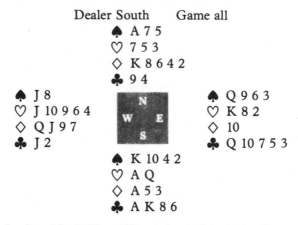

♠ A 7 5
♡ 7 5 3
◇ K 8 6 4 2
♣ 9 4

♠ J 8
♡ J 10 9 6 4
◇ Q J 9 7
♣ J 2

♠ Q 9 6 3
♡ K 8 2
◇ 10
♣ Q 10 7 5 3

♠ K 10 4 2
♡ A Q
◇ A 5 3
♣ A K 8 6

South played in 3NT and West's lead of the jack of hearts ran to the queen. At a table where I was watching, South played ace of diamonds and a second diamond, on which West played a slightly deceptive queen. The declarer ducked in dummy, East discarded a club, and the hearts were cleared. It was impossible now for South to develop a ninth trick.

You see where the declarer went wrong? There was no point at all in ducking the second round of diamonds; it was just force of habit, a standard communication play when communication was no worry. If he wins with the king he discovers the distribution and has time to play for three tricks in spades.

There was no swing on the board and later I asked the declarer at the other table how he had played 3NT. 'I won the heart lead', he said, 'and played two rounds of diamonds – ace and king. When they broke 4–1 I led a spade from dummy and put in the ten; the best chance seemed to be to find East with Q J x x.'

There he showed a slight lack of technical – or mathematical – knowledge. If the spades are 4–2 West is more likely to hold J x or Q x than x x. There are eight variations of the doubleton honour, only six of the plain doubleton. Also, leading low to the 10 loses unnecessarily when West has a singleton queen or jack; thus low to the king, back to the ace, and a third round from dummy, represents the best chance of landing three spade tricks.

20

Easy Pick-up

'Eight ever, nine never' is an old catch-phrase, implying that when a declarer who is missing the queen of trumps holds eight cards he should finesse for the queen, but when he holds nine he should play for the drop. There is not a lot in this, even as catch-phrases go, because the odds in favour of playing in a particular way are slight and there is usually a clue of some kind. For example, suppose you have this combination:

```
              A 6
Q 3                    8 7 4
         K J 10 9 5 2
```

You play ace and another, on which East may play any variety of his three low cards. However, West's three on the first round may be highly significant, because many players with a combination such as 8 3 or 7 3 will play the higher card on the first round. Since those combinations are now excluded, there is much to be said for going up with the king.

Another way of finding a missing queen – is not to look for it!

```
                    ♠ A J 8 2
                    ♡ Q 10 4
                    ◇ 4 3
                    ♣ K 9 6 2
♠ Q 7 3                              ♠ 5
♡ K 8 6            N                 ♡ A J 5 3
◇ 6 5 2        W       E             ◇ K J 10 9 7
♣ 10 7 4 3        S                  ♣ Q J 8
                    ♠ K 10 9 6 4
                    ♡ 9 7 2
                    ◇ A Q 8
                    ♣ A 5
```

East was the dealer and the bidding went:

South	West	North	East
—	—	—	1♦
1♠	No	2♦	No
2NT	No	4♠	No
No	No		

North's two diamonds meant, initially, that he had a fair raise in spades.

West led a diamond to South's queen. You can see what would happen to most players in this contract. They would cash the ace and king of spades – no reason to finesse – and in due course lose a trump and three hearts, for one down.

It is the sort of hand where an expert would play differently and the difference would hardly be noticed. South ruffed the third club and the third diamond, then led the fourth club from dummy and ruffed again. He exited with a heart and his last three cards were ♠ K 10 9 opposite dummy's A J 8.

You see, it's not always right to draw trumps.

Part II – Mainly Defence

Deals 21 – 41

21

Small Protest

The thought contained in this deal is not new – the idea has been around for 40 years or so – but there are many less well known extensions.

Deal South   N–S vulnerable

         ♠ K 10 9
         ♡ 6 5 2
         ◇ Q J 4
         ♣ A 7 5 3

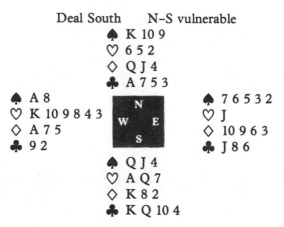

♠ A 8   ♠ 7 6 5 3 2
♡ K 10 9 8 4 3   ♡ J
◇ A 7 5   ◇ 10 9 6 3
♣ 9 2   ♣ J 8 6

         ♠ Q J 4
         ♡ A Q 7
         ◇ K 8 2
         ♣ K Q 10 4

In a pairs event South opens with a strong notrump and the bidding continues:

South	West	North	East
1NT	2♡	3♡	No
3NT	No	No	No

North's three hearts is a type of call that is much overdone, but here it seems the best choice. The score makes a double unattractive and a jump to 3NT might lead to a silly contract. If South has no firm guard in hearts he will name his best suit and North is not obliged to continue.

The lead of ♡ 10 is covered by the jack and queen. At trick two South tries the jack of spades. If this passes by unscathed he will switch to diamonds, with nine tricks guaranteed. But West wins, clears the hearts, and holds the declarer to eight tricks.

Did I hear a small protest? Correct, West should lead the king of hearts, not a low one. Anything else? Yes, as the play began, South should have allowed East's jack of hearts to hold the first trick. West surely has a six-card suit for his overcall, so the jack of hearts is sure to be a singleton.

Whenever the opening leader has two sure entry cards and knows that his partner can hold very little, he should allow for partner holding a singleton honour. The king may be right from K J 10 x x x, the ace from A J 10 x x x, even the queen from Q 10 9 x x x. When holding just one critical entry it may be right to lead the top card from such as A K 10 9 x x or A Q 10 9 x x; this will gain when partner has a singleton queen or king and the declarer J x x x.

22

Too Revealing

There are moments at the bridge table, as in life, when the slightest hesitation may be disastrous. This was one of them:

Dealer South   Game all

        ♠ Q J 6 2
        ♡ 10 5
        ◇ A 8 5 2
        ♣ K 6 2

♠ K 7   ♠ 9 8 3
♡ 9 6   ♡ A K J 8 7 3
◇ Q 10 7 4 3   ◇ J 6
♣ Q 10 8 3   ♣ 7 5

        ♠ A 10 5 4
        ♡ Q 4 2
        ◇ K 9
        ♣ A J 9 4

South opened one club and the bidding continued:

South	West	North	East
1♣	No	1◇	1♡
1♠	No	4♠	No
No	No		

North's raise to four spades may seem on the forward side, but his partner had made a free rebid and it seemed as though the top cards were in the right place.

West led the 9 of hearts, and after cashing the ace and king East played a third round to kill the discard on the queen. After a moment's thought West ruffed with the seven and dummy

[52]

overruffed.

That moment's thought was fatal. Judging that West had ruffed from K x, South played a spade to the ace, dropping the king. This left:

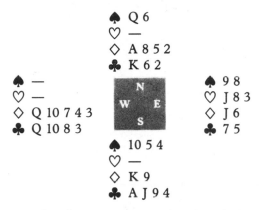

Two rounds of trumps were played and West was under pressure. He discarded two diamonds and South established his tenth trick by ruffing a diamond.

If West had ruffed the third heart with the king of spades South would have discarded a club from dummy, ruffed a club, and squeezed West in the minor suits. Nor would it help to discard on the heart; the only good play was to ruff with the seven, giving nothing away.

Test for Three

This was a very ordinary type of hand, where the play in notrumps would depend entirely on the relative skill of the three players concerned. The heart suit looks very ordinary too, but the play centres on just this one suit.

Dealer South   Game all

```
                  ♠ K 5
                  ♡ Q 10 6 5
                  ◇ Q 10 7 6
                  ♣ K 9 6
♠ Q 10 8 7 3        N         ♠ J 9 4
♡ A 8 4          W     E      ♡ 9 3 2
◇ 9 3               S         ◇ A 4 2
♣ 8 4 3                       ♣ Q J 7 2
                  ♠ A 6 2
                  ♡ K J 7
                  ◇ K J 8 5
                  ♣ A 10 5
```

As I expect I have mentioned elsewhere, I think it's silly to employ the old Stayman on the North hand. However, the bidding would normally go:

South	West	North	East
1NT	No	2♣	No
2◇	No	3NT	No
No	No		

West leads the 7 of spades. South ducks the first round and wins the second round on the table. He sees that he must knock out both red aces to make nine tricks. Moreover, if the spades are 5–3, which is likely, he must knock out West's ace first.

There is no way of telling which ace West is more likely to hold, but we will say that South leads a heart from dummy and puts on the king.

Now a moderate player in the West position would put on the ace, following the principle that a high card should be used to kill the opponent's high card. Of course, this ruins the defence, because after the spades have been cleared West has no further entry.

A better player in the West position will play low on the heart lead, but he may be a little slow or, more likely, a little fast. A clever South may draw the right conclusion.

An expert defender will play low at normal speed, giving the declarer no clue. Now all will depend on South's astuteness and also on his estimate of the opposition. The point is that a good player in East's place would not have failed to go up with the ace of hearts if he held it, to protect partner's entry. So when East (presumed to know what he is doing) does *not* go up with the ace of hearts there is a strong presumption that he does not hold it. In a battle between good players, therefore, South, having picked the right suit to play first, will continue hearts until he has forced out the ace.

24

A Disarming Reply

The player who trumped his partner's ace is a stock figure like the guardsman who dropped his rifle but, as all bridge players know, there are occasions when this traditional gaffe is the right play. This was one of the occasions, but the blame was not all on one side.

Dealer South   Love all

```
                  ♠ 10 8 6 4 2
                  ♡ 10 5
                  ◇ A Q J 2
                  ♣ J 6
  ♠ 3                              ♠ 9 5
  ♡ A Q              N             ♡ 9 8 6 4 2
  ◇ 9 7 5         W     E          ◇ 10 8 6 4 3
  ♣ A K 9 8 7 5 3     S            ♣ 2
                  ♠ A K Q J 7
                  ♡ K J 7 3
                  ◇ K
                  ♣ Q 10 4
```

The bidding went:

South	West	North	East
1♠	3♣	3♠	No
4♠	No	No	No

West led the king of clubs, which brought forth the six, two and ten, and followed with the ace of clubs, on which East discarded the two of hearts. A third club was ruffed by dummy's ten of spades and the declarer had no problem: three hearts went away on the high diamonds, and just one heart was lost.

'If you couldn't overruff the dummy, why didn't you ruff the second club and lead a heart up to the weakness?' demanded West.

'You know I'm not clever enough to do anything like that' was East's disarming reply.

West did indeed know that. With a partner who was not too bright, he should have taken charge of the defence by leading the nine of clubs at trick two, not the ace. Would this be dangerous? Of course not, although the point is often missed. With nine cards in view, it is clear that East's two of clubs is either a singleton or from Q 2 or from Q 10 2; in any of these cases it is safe for West to underlead the ace at trick two.

Suppose for a moment that East had held the four of clubs and declarer the Q 10 2. It would then be essential for declarer to play the ten, making it dangerous for West to underlead the ace, perhaps finding his partner with a doubleton 4 2. These are tricky situations and the declarer must be ready to play the 'right' card without any evident consideration.

25

Naughty Nineties

Two puzzles arise from the play of this deal in 3NT.

Dealer South　　Love all

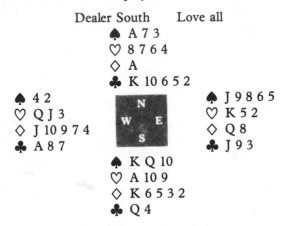

　　　　　　♠ A 7 3
　　　　　　♡ 8 7 6 4
　　　　　　♢ A
　　　　　　♣ K 10 6 5 2

♠ 4 2　　　　　　　　　　　♠ J 9 8 6 5
♡ Q J 3　　　　　　　　　　♡ K 5 2
♢ J 10 9 7 4　　　　　　　♢ Q 8
♣ A 8 7　　　　　　　　　　♣ J 9 3

　　　　　　♠ K Q 10
　　　　　　♡ A 10 9
　　　　　　♢ K 6 5 3 2
　　　　　　♣ Q 4

This was the bidding in an American tournament:

South	West	North	East
1 ♢	No	1 ♡ (1)	No
1NT	No	3NT (2)	No
No	No		

(1) There are those, heaven help us, who consider it a duty never to suppress a four-card suit at the one-level.

(2) Close between 2NT and 3NT; the five-card suit is an asset, the singleton ace a debit.

The first puzzle: How did South, after the diamond lead, make an overtrick in his contract of 3NT, with only the tiniest misplay by a defender?

Answer: He won the jack of diamonds in dummy, East unblocking the queen, and led the two of clubs, on which East played the nine, South the queen, and West (smoothly) the seven. Then he led the four of clubs to the *king*. A third round cleared the suit, and that was ten tricks.

Second puzzle: What was the defensive misplay?

Answer: *Not* West's duck; this was correct play, giving East the chance to win the next club and return a diamond while West still had an entry. The slip was *East's*, in playing the nine of clubs at trick two. South reflected that the nine would be abnormal play from A 9 x, but normal from J 9 x.

This was a clever deduction, leading to some interesting thoughts. With A 9 x or K 9 x it is often good play to put in the nine.

For example:

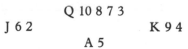

$$\begin{array}{ccc} & \text{Q 10 8 7 3} & \\ \text{J 6 2} & & \text{K 9 4} \\ & \text{A 5} & \end{array}$$

When South leads the ace (or low from dummy) East must drop the nine. This will surely induce declarer to play the queen on the next round, because if East has J 9 alone four tricks can be established. To find East with K 9 is not so helpful, because a trick must still be lost to the jack.

26

As Others See Us

A few years ago the Bulletin of the American Contract Bridge League reported (in all seriousness) that the Interim Catalog of Sullins College, Bristol, Va., offered a course of Duplicate Bridge with J. Darrell Kennedy as faculty sponsor. The course was described as 'a study of deductive reasoning, nonparametric statistics, and sensitivity of others, using duplicate bridge as a vehicle.' Could P.G. Wodehouse have done better? But who knows, the instruction might be useful on a deal like this:

Dealer South   Game all

```
                 ♠ Q 8
                 ♡ J 6
                 ◇ K Q 10 8 5 3
                 ♣ A 7 4
♠ K J 7 5                        ♠ A 9 2
♡ Q 10 7 5 2          N         ♡ 9 8 4
◇ A 2            W        E      ◇ 7 6 4
♣ 9 6                S           ♣ J 10 5 3
                 ♠ 10 6 4 3
                 ♡ A K 3
                 ◇ J 9
                 ♣ K Q 8 2
```

The bidding goes:

South	West	North	East
1♣	No	1◇	No
1NT	No	3NT	No
No	No		

Sitting West, you lead your fourth best heart, the jack is played from dummy, and South quite shrewdly overtakes with the king. His idea is to create the impression that he has A K alone; this may divert the opponents from switching the attack to spades.

When diamonds are led you win the second round, and this is the moment to put on your nonparametric thinking-cap. Eight tricks are in view and declarer must surely hold either ace of spades or king of clubs.

You can't just sit there and play patty-cake in a situation of this sort. There is positively no chance of beating the contract unless partner holds the ace of spades. Displaying sensitivity to others, you lead not the fourth best but the king of spades, because this wins not only when partner holds A 10 x but also when he holds A 9 x. He unblocks the nine and now you can run four tricks in the suit. It takes two to tango, as they say.

27

Strange Partners

On this deal from a pairs contest the lazy players and the good players did the same thing, while those in between played a different defence. Imagine that you hold the West cards. I will give you the advantage of a good partner.

Dealer South   N–S vulnerable

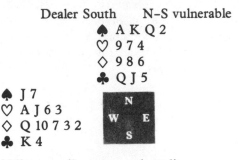

♠ A K Q 2
♡ 9 7 4
◇ 9 8 6
♣ Q J 5

♠ J 7
♡ A J 6 3
◇ Q 10 7 3 2
♣ K 4

The bidding usually went on these lines:

South	North
1♣	1♠
1NT	3NT
No	

Your lead of the three of diamonds goes to the jack and king. The declarer crosses to dummy with a spade, on which partner plays the three. On the queen of clubs East plays the seven and you win with the king. What next?

It is safe to continue diamonds, with the ace of hearts as entry, but is there not a danger that declarer will run for home before you regain the lead? Some players in the pairs event took that view. There was room for partner to hold the king of hearts, they reflected, so they switched to a low heart, hoping to take four heart tricks.

The good players saw a little more deeply into the position. South was going to make three tricks in spades (East's three suggesting an odd number, doubtless five) and two in diamonds. What about the clubs? Partner's seven looked like the beginning of an echo, showing an even number. So South had only eight tricks on top! Play passive, therefore, and clear the diamonds. This was the full hand:

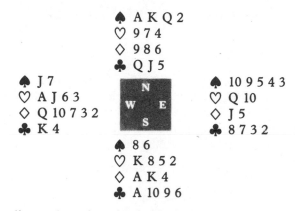

♠ A K Q 2
♡ 9 7 4
◇ 9 8 6
♣ Q J 5

♠ J 7
♡ A J 6 3
◇ Q 10 7 3 2
♣ K 4

♠ 10 9 5 4 3
♡ Q 10
◇ J 5
♣ 8 7 3 2

♠ 8 6
♡ K 8 5 2
◇ A K 4
♣ A 10 9 6

The diamond continuation holds declarer to eight tricks. Many players overdo signalling in defence, but this was an occasion when East could judge that the three of spades and the seven of clubs would help his partner and not the declarer.

28

Second Best Choice

Supposing that you were too strong for 1NT not vulnerable, what would you open on the North hand below? If you play five-card majors you have to open one club. Otherwise, one heart is better than one spade; over a response of two clubs or two diamonds you can rebid in notrumps, concealing the spades.

Dealer North   E–W vulnerable

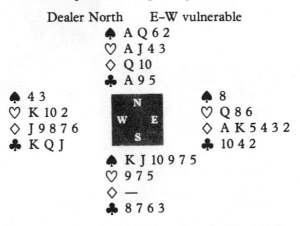

```
                    ♠ A Q 6 2
                    ♡ A J 4 3
                    ◇ Q 10
                    ♣ A 9 5
  ♠ 4 3                              ♠ 8
  ♡ K 10 2             N             ♡ Q 8 6
  ◇ J 9 8 7 6      W       E         ◇ A K 5 4 3 2
  ♣ K Q J              S             ♣ 10 4 2
                    ♠ K J 10 9 7 5
                    ♡ 9 7 5
                    ◇ —
                    ♣ 8 7 6 3
```

On this occasion South held the spade suit. The bidding went:

South	West	North	East
—	—	1♡	No
1♠	No	3♠	No
4♠	No	No	No

South won the club lead in dummy, ruffed a diamond, drew two rounds of trumps, and ruffed the other diamond. Then he exited with a club, hoping that something favourable would happen in the heart suit. West cashed his club tricks, leaving:

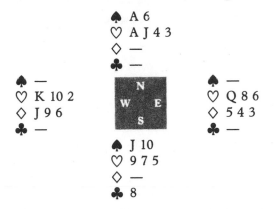

♠ A 6
♡ A J 4 3
◇ —
♣ —

♠ —
♡ K 10 2
◇ J 9 6
♣ —

♠ —
♡ Q 8 6
◇ 5 4 3
♣ —

♠ J 10
♡ 9 7 5
◇ —
♣ 8

West advanced the ten of hearts and the jack was headed by the queen. East returned the six of hearts and now South took the right view, playing the seven and forcing West's king.

'We could have beaten this contract if you had held Q 8 7 of hearts instead of Q 8 6,' West remarked.

'You don't need to find me with Q 8 7,' East replied. 'Q 8 5 is enough. You must lead the king, not the ten.' (And similarly, if of course, in West's position, the queen from Q 10 x.)

29

'What Happens If . . .'

'What happens if. . . ,' among tournament players, is a phrase that generally means: 'You idiot, why didn't you. . . ?' And that was the meaning of West's remark at the conclusion of this deal.

Dealer North   N–S vulnerable

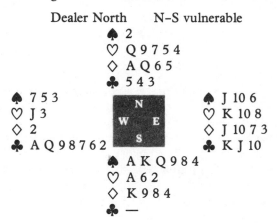

```
              ♠ 2
              ♡ Q 9 7 5 4
              ◇ A Q 6 5
              ♣ 5 4 3
♠ 7 5 3                      ♠ J 10 6
♡ J 3                        ♡ K 10 8
◇ 2                          ◇ J 10 7 3
♣ A Q 9 8 7 6 2              ♣ K J 10
              ♠ A K Q 9 8 4
              ♡ A 6 2
              ◇ K 9 8 4
              ♣ —
```

South opened one spade and the bidding continued:

South	West	North	East
1♠	2♣	Dble(1)	No
2◇	No	3◇	No
3♠	No	4◇	No
6◇	No	No	No

(1) A negative double, implying initially fair values with no obvious alternative. It worked well here, in the sense that it helped the partnership to arrive at a contract in diamonds.

South ruffed the club lead, then played king and ace of diamonds, discovering the trump division. He ruffed another club, then played the top spades, arriving at this position:

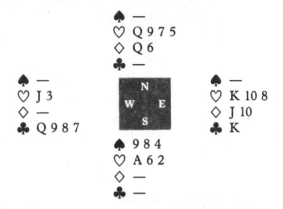

East ruffed the next spade and exited with a club. Dummy ruffed and drew the last trump. Now South held just the ace of hearts and winning spades.

There was a silence until West said: 'I think we might have beaten that somehow. What happens if you lead the king of hearts after you have ruffed the spade?'

30

Stranded

It is strange, in a way, that when the dummy is weak a defender will always note the lack of entries and conspire against them, but when the dummy is strong it may not occur to him that perhaps the declarer is short of entries. Consider this deal from a match between England and Scotland in the Camrose series.

Dealer West   E–W vulnerable

```
                ♠ 10 8
                ♡ A Q 9 5
                ♢ Q J 6 2
                ♣ A 7 5
♠ A 5                              ♠ Q 6 4
♡ K J 8 7 6         N              ♡ 4 3
♢ A 4          W         E         ♢ K 10 7 5 3
♣ Q 10 4 3          S              ♣ K J 2
                ♠ K J 9 7 3 2
                ♡ 10 2
                ♢ 9 8
                ♣ 9 8 6
```

The distinguished partnership of Tony Priday and Claude Rodrigue held the North–South cards. This was the bidding:

South	West	North	East
—	1♡	No	1NT
2♠	No	2NT	No
3♠	No	No	No

Non-playing captain of the English side, I had advised Rodrigue (South) not to bid on nothing; in vain.

West led a low heart – by no means an inspired choice. Declarer won in dummy with the nine and ran the ten of spades to West's ace. West exited with a club, and Claude was able to draw trumps, finesse the queen of hearts, and make nine tricks.

The commentator on Vu-Graph remarked simply that South must have been surprised to make the contract. Certainly a club lead would have defeated it, but the defence had another chance. Suppose West declines to win the first round of spades: a second spade goes to the ace and now the defence plays a club. Declarer wins the second round and this is the position:

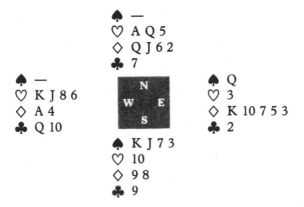

South is stranded in dummy, unable to gain entry for the heart finesse.

31

Half Truth

'When the opening leader has four or five trumps,' I read in somebody's book recently, 'he should lead from his longest suit, forcing declarer to ruff and so gaining control of the trump situation.'

Like most generalities about bridge, this one is right only half the time. It may be right, for example, when the bidding suggests that the trumps against you are 5-3 or 5-2; but when they are likely to be 5-4 or 4-4, it will not hurt the declarer to take several ruffs.

Another time when it is a mistake to play a forcing game is when you hold long and fairly strong trumps and the declarer is marked with a much longer suit. Now your principal aim should be to avoid being end-played in the trump suit and so losing your natural trump tricks.

Dealer North   Game all

♠ —
♡ K Q J
♢ A Q J 6 4 2
♣ J 8 6 5

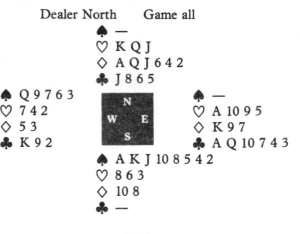

♠ Q 9 7 6 3
♡ 7 4 2
♢ 5 3
♣ K 9 2

♠ —
♡ A 10 9 5
♢ K 9 7
♣ A Q 10 7 4 3

♠ A K J 10 8 5 4 2
♡ 8 6 3
♢ 10 8
♣ —

[70]

The bidding went:

South	West	North	East
—	—	1 ◇	2 ♣
4 ♠	No	No	No

West began with the king of clubs. South ruffed, cashed the ace of spades, and switched to a heart. East won and returned a heart, but he could not prevent South from ruffing two more clubs and arriving at this end position:

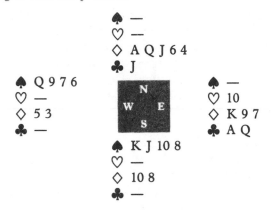

South exited with ace and another diamond. It was easy for him now to make three of the last four tricks.

To preserve his trump tricks, West should have begun with his shortest suit, diamonds. Then South would have no play for the contract.

32

No Cause for Dancing

There are occasions in bridge when it is right to offer the opponents a little encouragement. Alas, this is seldom done from kindness of heart. The idea is to show them a faint light that may lead them onward to a much worse fate. The deceptive play made by West on this deal was rare but devastating.

Dealer South   N–S vulnerable

```
                    ♠ 8 7 5
                    ♡ A Q 10 8 4
                    ◇ J 4
                    ♣ Q 7 3
♠ A J 10 4                          ♠ Q
♡ 7 3                  N            ♡ J 9 6 5 2
◇ K Q 10 8 6 2    W       E         ◇ A 9 7 5
♣ 10                  S            ♣ 9 8 5
                    ♠ K 9 6 3 2
                    ♡ K
                    ◇ 3
                    ♣ A K J 6 4 2
```

The bidding went:

South	West	North	East
1♣	1◇	1♡	3◇
3♠	No	4♠	No
No	Dble	No	No
No			

The raise to four spades was very questionable. North should have taken into account that his partner might have stretched to bid over three diamonds. It is one of the follies of the modern style that too many bids are treated as forcing.

The defence to four spades doubled began with two rounds of diamonds. South ruffed, overtook the king of hearts with the ace, and led a spade from the table, on which East's queen appeared. Afraid of finding West with A J 10 x, South refrained from covering the queen with the king, and now West made a clever play, dropping the ten.

'Not so bad as it might have been,' thought South to himself. 'East has Q x and West A J 10. I shall be only one down.'

When East, in with the queen of spades, led a club to dummy's queen, South played another spade from the table, and now the roof came down. West won with the jack, cashed the ace, and followed with a diamond. South made only two more tricks – one trump and, eventually, the queen of hearts.

If the ten of spades had not appeared on the first round of trumps, South would not have risked leading another round and so losing the tempo. He would simply have continued clubs, letting the defence make three trump tricks for two down and a penalty of 500. No cause for dancing in the streets, but better than 1400.

33

False Impression

When partner makes a bright opening lead against a notrump contract – it does happen sometimes – there is quite an art in concealing the situation from the declarer. The object, of course, is to give declarer the wrong idea about who has length in the dangerous suit. East managed to do just that on the following hand:

```
          Dealer south      N–S vulnerable
                    ♠ A 8 3 2
                    ♡ 7 4
                    ◇ K J 10 8 4
                    ♣ Q 9
    ♠ K 7 6 4                         ♠ Q 9
    ♡ Q J 3          N               ♡ K 10 8 6 5
    ◇ 9 6         W     E            ◇ Q 3
    ♣ J 8 4 2         S              ♣ 10 6 5 3
                    ♠ J 10 5
                    ♡ A 9 2
                    ◇ A 7 5 2
                    ♣ A K 7
```

The bidding went:

South	West	North	East
1NT(1)	No	2♣(2)	No
2◇	No	3NT	No
No	No		

(1) 15–17 on this occasion.

(2) Every time you look at a bridge magazine, or a match record, you will see Stayman responses on this type of hand. I can see two

good reasons against it: (a) North has enough for a raise to 3NT without giving information to the opponents; (b) even if partner has four spades it is doubtful whether four spades will be a better contract than 3NT, where the strong diamond suit will carry weight. (Remember that for four spades to make, 3NT to fail, you need to make not one, but two, more tricks in the suit contract.)

Having been informed that South did not hold a four-card major, West struck the good lead of the queen of hearts. As his only hope of gaining entry to cash the long hearts lay in the queen of diamonds, East attempted to create the impression that his partner held the long hearts and that his hand was 'harmless'. He played the eight of hearts on the opening lead, overtook the jack with the king, and returned the five.

It looked to South as though West had led from Q J 10 x x and that East held K 8 5. Falling into the trap, he won the third heart and took a diamond finesse into the 'safe' hand. This way, he lost four hearts and a diamond. Clearly, if East had played the normal cards in hearts, South would have managed the diamonds more successfully.

34

Through the Slips

It is always a little humiliating, when defending against 3NT, to take a trick in the middle of the play and fail to cash four more that are immediately available. Normally there is some indication pointing to the right play. See what you think of this hand from a team-of-four match.

Dealer West   Game all

♠ K 5
♡ 6
◇ J 9 4
♣ A K J 10 8 3 2

♠ J 10 7 4 3		♠ Q 9 6 2
♡ Q J 8 3	N	♡ A K 4 2
◇ K 2	W E	◇ 8 5
♣ 9 4	S	♣ Q 7 6

♠ A 8
♡ 10 9 7 5
◇ A Q 10 7 6 3
♣ 5

This was the bidding at the first table:

South	West	North	East
—	No	1♣	No
1◇	No	2♣	No
2♡	No	3♣	No
3NT	No	No	No

West led a low spade, which went to the queen and ace. The

declarer cashed two clubs, then ran the jack of diamonds, which lost to West's king. West played another spade and South was home with five diamonds and four top cards in the black suits.

'He had bid hearts', said West. 'I could hardly place you with the ace and king, especially as I held Q J myself.'

This was in no way an intelligent remark. West should have thought along these lines:

'Declarer's play of the ace and king of clubs is not the normal way to tackle such a combination. It is plain that he was giving himself a chance to run this suit before testing the diamonds. If he had held a guard in hearts he would have played on diamonds first. Alternatively, he might have won the spade with the ace and forced out the queen of clubs.'

When in doubt, ask yourself what declarer would be doing if he held certain cards. That is what defence is about.

At the other table North–South did well to reach five diamonds. After 1 ♣ – 1 ◇ – 2 ♣ South bid 2NT; then North showed diamond support and the final contract became obvious.

35

Hippo Dancing

Many years ago I described 5NT as the 'hippopotamus contract', awkward and ungainly. I have noticed that it often leads to something unusual in the play.

Dealer South   Game all

                  ♠ J 8 6 4
                  ♡ A K 10 5 3
                  ◇ 8
                  ♣ 9 4 3

♠ 10 7 5 2   ♠ A 9 3
♡ —   ♡ J 9 8 6 2
◇ Q 10 9 5 4 3   ◇ A J 7 2
♣ 10 8 6   ♣ 2

                  ♠ K Q
                  ♡ Q 7 4
                  ◇ K 6
                  ♣ A K Q J 7 5

Many players would open 2NT on the South hand, but South was content with one club and the bidding continued:

South	West	North	East
1♣	No	1♡	No
3NT	No	4♣	No
4♡	No	5◇	No
5NT	No	No	No

North was right to make one forward move over 3NT, but he should have given up over four hearts or, at most, have bid 4NT.

West led the ten of diamonds and East made a critical play on the first trick, playing the seven, not the ace. The ace would be a mistake if South held K Q x, and if he held K x or K x x the timing for the defence would be easier after the play of the low diamond.

After five rounds of clubs the position was:

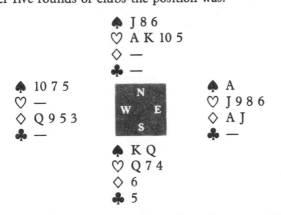

On the last club East was able to discard the ace of diamonds. South made the top hearts but had to concede the last three tricks.

If East takes the ace of diamonds at trick one the defence becomes impossible. His last five cards will be ace of spades and four hearts, and he will easily be end-played.

36

Half Measures

'We have scotched the snake, not killed it,' murmured a literary-minded player in the middle of the deal below. In bridge terms, West recognized the opportunity for a well-known defensive coup but was half-hearted in its execution.

Dealer North   E–W vulnerable

    ♠ 7 4 3
    ♡ A 9 5
    ◇ J 10 9 6 5 3
    ♣ 5

♠ J 9 6 5   ♠ 10 8 2
♡ Q 8 3 2   ♡ K 7 4
◇ A Q   ◇ 7 4 2
♣ Q 6 2   ♣ J 9 8 4

    ♠ A K Q
    ♡ J 10 6
    ◇ K 8
    ♣ A K 10 7 3

Most players could bear to pass on the North hand, but this North, in view of the score, was impelled to open three diamonds. The bidding continued:

South	West	North	East
—	—	3◇	No
3NT	No	No	No

Do you like South's 3NT? It might have been right if North had held three losers in hearts, but it would be wrong if he held short hearts or perhaps A x of hearts and a loser in diamonds. South might have tried three spades, but I like five diamonds just as well.

Against 3NT, West led a spade to the ten and king. The king of diamonds was taken by the ace and West, knowing from the play to the first trick that South held the top spades, switched to a low heart. Clearly it was necessary to attack dummy's entry for the diamonds.

The declarer played low from dummy and East put on the king. South was careful to unblock the ten. East returned a heart and now South played the jack. West did not cover, but dummy's ace of hearts was later an entry for the established diamonds.

When West was in with the ace of diamonds he should have led the queen of hearts, not a low one. South may play the ace and unblock the ten from hand, but he can be kept out of dummy afterwards.

The lead of the queen of hearts is a type of play usually described as a Deschapelles Coup. More exactly, it is a Merrimac Coup. The Deschapelles, if one is to be historically accurate, is a sacrificial play that creates an entry to partner's hand.

37

Voice of Thunder

In general, it is a mistake in defence to leave yourself with a minor tenace (J x against an opponent's Q 10) instead of a major tenace (A J over Q 10). It is more difficult for the declarer to negotiate an endplay when the opponents hold major tenaces than when they hold minor tenaces. West learned a bitter lesson on this deal from rubber bridge.

```
                  Dealer South      Love all
                     ♠ K 6 4
                     ♡ A J 10 7
                     ◇ J 9 4
                     ♣ A 7 3
    ♠ A Q 10 9                         ♠ 7
    ♡ Q 9 6          N                 ♡ K 8 5 3 2
    ◇ 10 7 5 2    W     E              ◇ 8
    ♣ 6 2            S                 ♣ K Q 10 9 5 4
                     ♠ J 8 5 3 2
                     ♡ 4
                     ◇ A K Q 6 3
                     ♣ J 8
```

The South hand is an awkward type. Whether one spade is better than one diamond (or a pass) is debatable. South on this occasion opened one spade. North responded 3NT, and South tried four diamonds. When North amended to four spades, West doubled in a voice of thunder.

West led a club, won by the queen, and East returned his singleton diamond. South went up with the ace and led a low spade. West could have played low and been sure of three tricks, but instead he played the ace. Then, having decided that his partner could hardly hold another trump, he led another club.

South now retrieved his venturesome bidding with accurate play. Three rounds of hearts and three more diamonds led to:

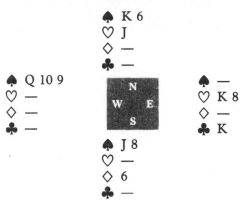

```
              ♠ K 6
              ♡ J
              ◇ —
              ♣ —
♠ Q 10 9                      ♠ —
♡ —          ┌─────────┐      ♡ K 8
◇ —          │    N    │      ◇ —
♣ —          │ W     E │      ♣ K
             │    S    │
             └─────────┘
              ♠ J 8
              ♡ —
              ◇ 6
              ♣ —
```

West had to ruff the next diamond and concede the last two tricks.

'The way you doubled, I thought they were going four down,' said East unkindly.

'There was nothing wrong with my double,' replied West with dignity. 'I made a slight error in the play, that's all.'

38

Indian Rope Trick

Whether you play bridge in New York, London, Hong Kong, or
Timbuktu, it is fairly certain that you have heard of the resourceful
Pakistani, Zia Mahmood. Zia thinks of odd little plays that simply
don't occur to anyone else. He plays most of his bridge in the
London clubs and one day he showed me this deal:

Dealer West   Game all

```
                  ♠ Q 10 5 2
                  ♡ 10 5 4
                  ◇ A Q J
                  ♣ A K J
    ♠ A 4                         ♠ J 9 3
    ♡ A K Q 8 2      N            ♡ 7 6 3
    ◇ K 10 4 3    W     E         ◇ 9 8 6
    ♣ 7 3            S            ♣ 9 6 5 4
                  ♠ K 8 7 6
                  ♡ J 9
                  ◇ 7 5 2
                  ♣ Q 10 8 2
```

'I was East,' he said, 'with the sort of hand you say you generally
hold.' The bidding went:

South	West	North	East
—	1♡	Dble	No
1♠	No	3♠	No
4♠	No	No	No

'Do you see any way to beat this contract?'
'You start with three rounds of hearts, I suppose,' I said a little

doubtfully. 'But South ought to get the spades right.'

'Yes, I played high-low in hearts and partner played a third round. South ruffed and played a low spade to the queen.' He ticked off the cards.

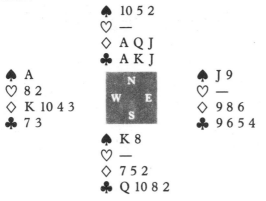

```
              ♠ 10 5 2
              ♡ —
              ◇ A Q J
              ♣ A K J
♠ A                          ♠ J 9
♡ 8 2                        ♡ —
◇ K 10 4 3                   ◇ 9 8 6
♣ 7 3                        ♣ 9 6 5 4
              ♠ K 8
              ♡ —
              ◇ 7 5 2
              ♣ Q 10 8 2
```

Now I saw the point. When a spade came back, Zia inserted the *jack*. You see the effect of that? South happily covered the jack with the king. West won and after an agonizing pause led a fourth heart, promoting a trick for Zia's nine of spades.

39

Urgent Message

Most of us complain of our partners from time to time, even when we suspect that we may have contributed to the error. This was a typical occasion at rubber bridge where East was full of grief, not realizing that he could have saved the ship.

Dealer South   Game all

```
                    ♠ J 6 5 3 2
                    ♡ K J 6 4
                    ◇ A
                    ♣ J 8 3
♠ 10 8                              ♠ Q
♡ A 7                               ♡ Q 10 8 5 3 2
◇ K Q 7 6 5 4 3 2                   ◇ J 9 8
♣ 6                                 ♣ Q 10 9
                    ♠ A K 9 7 4
                    ♡ 9
                    ◇ 10
                    ♣ A K 7 5 4 2
```

The bidding went:

South	West	North	East
1♣	3◇	No(1)	No
3♠	No	4◇	No
5♠(2)	No	6♠	No
No	No		

(1) A tournament player would double at this point – not for penalties, but to show values.

[86]

(2) And at this point most tournament players would bid four hearts, to assure partner that they had a control in this suit. I see nothing wrong with five spades, emphasizing the quality of the black suits.

Against six spades West began with the king of diamonds. South won and drew two rounds of trumps, East discarding a low heart. The singleton heart came next and West, who had steeled himself for this moment, played low. Declarer naturally went up with the king. He lost a club trick later, but that was all.

'You knew he had a big two-suiter', grumbled East. 'What was the point of ducking the heart?'

'He could have been 5-2-1-5 with a doubleton heart and no loser in clubs', West replied. 'I didn't want to solve a possible guess.'

This was a fair answer and West might have carried the war to his partner. The point is that East, who had a sure club trick, knew more about the hand than West. On the second spade he should have thrown the heart queen, saying to partner, 'There's no guess in hearts: don't go to bed with the ace, whatever happens. You can rely on me for a second trick (a club).'

40

West Did Not Bite

Many books and articles describe clever traps that are set for the opposition, but not many have anything to say about how to avoid them. For that reason I liked the play of this deal from a team trial in Poland.

Dealer South   Game all

```
                ♠ 4 2
                ♡ 10 4 3
                ◇ A K J 9 8
                ♣ 10 7 2
♠ K 10 7 5 3                    ♠ J 8 6
♡ K 8              N             ♡ A Q 7 6 2
◇ 6 5 3        W       E         ◇ 4 2
♣ K 4 3            S             ♣ 8 6 5
                ♠ A Q 9
                ♡ J 9 5
                ◇ Q 10 7
                ♣ A Q J 9
```

If North–South are playing a weak notrump throughout, the bidding may go:

South	West	North	East
1♣	No	1◇	No
1NT	No	2NT	No
3NT	No	No	No

West leads a low spade and East contributes the jack. Many of the

South players recognized the opportunity for a standard deception. Intending to finesse a club into West's hand, they won the first trick with the *ace* of spades. The idea was that if West came in with a club he might read his partner for the queen of spades and lead a low one.

This plan worked at some tables, but not when the celebrated pair of Lebioda and Wilkosz held the East–West cards. Here South won the first trick with the ace of spades, led the ten of diamonds to the king, and ran the ten of clubs. Wilkosz won with the king and played – what, do you suppose?

Well, he laid down the king of spades. When his partner played a low spade he shifted resolutely to the king of hearts and so defeated the contract by two tricks.

Do you see why West led the king of spades and not a low one? He trusted his partner, with Q J x, to unblock the queen. When partner did not play the queen he placed South with this card. From there it was only a short journey to the conclusion that South had made the deceptive play in spades because he was wide open in hearts.

41

A Psychological Test

One of the recurring problems for the defending side is whether or not to lead the ace of an unbid suit against a small slam. You may be leading into the declarer's K x; on the other hand, he may have two top losers, and if you don't lead this ace you may never make it.

You have to listen to the bidding and try to decide whether, if you don't lead this suit, there is a danger of the losers being discarded. When the situation is not clear, my advice is to lead the ace. I am sure that many more contracts are made because an ace was *not* led than are made because it *was* led.

The problem is especially acute when you have a likely trick on the side. This hand from an international trial led to much heart-searching.

Dealer North   Love all

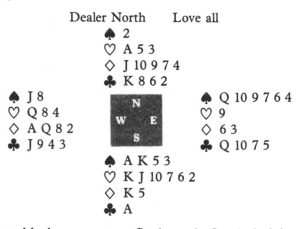

```
                 ♠ 2
                 ♡ A 5 3
                 ◇ J 10 9 7 4
                 ♣ K 8 6 2
♠ J 8                              ♠ Q 10 9 7 6 4
♡ Q 8 4            N               ♡ 9
◇ A Q 8 2      W     E             ◇ 6 3
♣ J 9 4 3         S               ♣ Q 10 7 5
                 ♠ A K 5 3
                 ♡ K J 10 7 6 2
                 ◇ K 5
                 ♣ A
```

At one table the contract was five hearts by South. A club was led and South made his contract by straightforward play. He ruffed two spades with dummy's low trumps, discarded one diamond on the king of clubs and lost just one trick to the queen of hearts and one to the ace of diamonds.

At the other table, where the team at that time known as 'The Aces' held the North–South cards, South opened a conventional one club, North responded one spade, showing three controls (two for an ace, one for a king), and the rest of the bidding was on natural lines. South finished in six hearts, having at one point shown a control in diamonds.

When West began with ace and another diamond the declarer thought to himself: 'Would West, after I had shown a control in diamonds, have led the ace, apparently from A Q? It looks as though he is hoping to make a trick with the queen of trumps.'

Having won with the king of diamonds, South immediately ran the jack of hearts. When this held he cashed the ace of clubs, ruffed a spade low, discarded his other spade on the king of clubs, and made the slam.

Is there a moral for the defence? I suppose that, against an astute opponent, it is unwise to lead an ace when you have *hopes* of a trump trick. Try something else and hope that both tricks will come your way.

Part III – Bidding Tactics

Deals 42 – 51

42

Thin on Top

On this deal from a match between Spain and Austria the same very expensive miscalculation was made at both tables. Let's see how it would strike you. You hold in the East position:

♠ K 8
♡ A 9 8 6
◇ A K 9 7
♣ K 5 3

South, on your left, is the dealer at game all and the bidding goes:

South	West	North	East
1♠	2♣	3♠	3NT
No	No	4♠	?

What do you do now? Double, did you say? Yes, well, that's what East did at both tables, though at the second table the bidding was slightly different, North raising to four spades on the first round. This was the full deal:

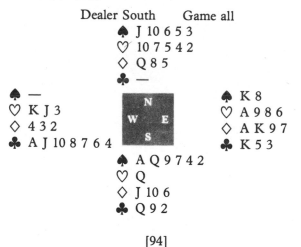

Dealer South   Game all
　　　　　　　♠ J 10 6 5 3
　　　　　　　♡ 10 7 5 4 2
　　　　　　　◇ Q 8 5
　　　　　　　♣ —

♠ —　　　　　　　　　　　♠ K 8
♡ K J 3　　　　　　　　　♡ A 9 8 6
◇ 4 3 2　　　　　　　　　◇ A K 9 7
♣ A J 10 8 7 6 4　　　　♣ K 5 3

　　　　　　　♠ A Q 9 7 4 2
　　　　　　　♡ Q
　　　　　　　◇ J 10 6
　　　　　　　♣ Q 9 2

West led the ace of clubs. With the king of spades marked by the bidding, South had no difficulty in making four spades doubled, scoring 790. East–West soon realized that they might have played in six clubs and scored 1390, as the cards lay. (It should be easy to pick up the clubs, because only a shortage in this suit would account for North's raise on what must be very slender values.)

The lesson in the deal is that when everyone is bidding away and you have a big hand, you must always support your partner to the limit before doubling the opposition. Since each of the other players must be thin in high cards, the distribution must be freakish and there is a considerable danger that aces and kings will go to waste in defence. After his partner had made a vulnerable overcall, East could have invited a slam with a bid of 4NT, and West, with his void in spades, might well have responded with a leap to six clubs; even if he bids only five clubs, a large number of points are saved.

43

Sure as Eggs is Eggs

We all fancy ourselves as psychologists at rubber bridge, thinking that we know how to handle bad partners as well as good ones. Some years ago I set a competition in the *Observer* where solvers were asked to imagine that they were playing with (a) a good partner, and (b) a bad one, who knows the basic conventions of bidding but makes all the standard errors. His play of the cards may be assumed to be reasonable. These were two of the problems:

1. At love all the bidding goes:

South	West	North	East
—	—	3♡	3♠
?			

South holds:

> ♠ Q 7 3
> ♡ 4
> ◇ K Q
> ♣ A K J 10 6 5 3

What should South call with (a) the good partner, (b) the bad one?

2. At game all the bidding goes:

South	West	North	East
—	—	—	1♣
Dble	No	1♠	No

South holds:

♠ K 10 7 4
♡ A J 9
♢ A Q 8 6 4
♣ 4

What should South call with (a) and with (b)?

Answer to 1: With a good partner it is reasonable to bid 3NT, partly because you may make it and partly because this may deter the opposition from going to four spades, which may be on for them. Four clubs (competitive) would not be a mistake but would give up the chance of game.

With a bad partner it would be most unwise to bid either 3NT or four clubs because, as sure as eggs is eggs, North will bid four hearts and sustain a penalty. You must pass.

Answer to 2: With a good partner a single raise to two spades is enough. He will advance on a moderate holding such as five spades to the queen and one of the red kings.

With a bad partner one has to exaggerate a little and bid three spades. The point is that with the South hand he would himself jump to three spades (if not to four). By the same token he will undervalue the North hand, failing to advance over two spades when he should. You must give him an extra push.

44

In Hot Water

'I never know,' wrote a correspondent, 'what is the right thing to do when opponents are bidding two suits and I hold one of them strongly. Is it right or wrong to double this suit? I got into hot water recently when at game all I held:

♠ K J 10 6 3
♡ 7
◇ 6 2
♣ K 9 8 4 2

'It was rubber bridge and the opponents were 40 up. My partner, North, opened one heart and the bidding went:

South	West	North	East
—	—	1♡	1♠
No	2◇	2♡	2♠
No	No	3♡	Dble
No	No	No	

'I didn't double two spades because I didn't want to drive them into diamonds. The full hand was something like this:

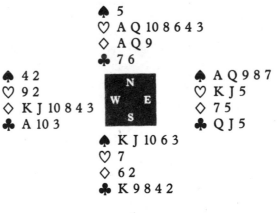

    ♠ 5
    ♡ A Q 10 8 6 4 3
    ◇ A Q 9
    ♣ 7 6

♠ 4 2   ♠ A Q 9 8 7
♡ 9 2   ♡ K J 5
◇ K J 10 8 4 3   ◇ 7 5
♣ A 10 3   ♣ Q J 5

    ♠ K J 10 6 3
    ♡ 7
    ◇ 6 2
    ♣ K 9 8 4 2

'My partner was very cross because three hearts went one down and we could have taken 500 or so from either two spades or three diamonds.'

Your partner was right. In general, when there has been a round or two of bidding, double what is under your nose, as it were. In my distant youth I once held in an international match:

♠ K J 10 8
♥ J 5 2
♦ K Q J 8 3
♣ 2

I was West and at game all the bidding went:

South	West	North	East
1♥	1♠	2♦	2♠
3♦	Dble	all pass	

I don't claim much credit for doubling three diamonds (which went for 500), but this is a situation where some players would have passed for fear of driving the enemy back to hearts. The reason why I remember the incident is that the ass then writing for the *Times* made a snide comment about my double.

The time to be careful is when partner has opened with a pre-emptive bid and an opponent has overcalled in a suit which you hold strongly. In this situation don't double unless you can double everything.

45

Shape Is Important

This deal from a match between the USA and Australia supports two of my theories about bidding. Sorry if you've heard them before!

First, I regard 4-4-4-1 as a defensive type. It will certainly be inconvenient for the opponents if they obtain the contract in any of your long suits. And there is another reason why I would be inclined to pass the West hand below.

<pre>
            Dealer West   Love all
                    ♠ 10 6 3
                    ♡ K J
                    ◇ K J 8 3
                    ♣ Q 9 8 4
    ♠ A   ♠ K 8 7
    ♡ 9 8 7 4   N   ♡ A 3
    ◇ A 10 7 2   W   E   ◇ 9 6 5 4
    ♣ A 10 6 2   S   ♣ K J 7 3
                    ♠ Q J 9 5 4 2
                    ♡ Q 10 6 5 2
                    ◇ Q
                    ♣ 5
</pre>

The second reason why I wouldn't mind passing on the West hand is that one of the aces is a singleton and may not carry much weight.

But it is, of course, normal to open a hand containing three aces and the American player, Robert Hamman, selected one heart. It was then more than likely that East-West would finish in 3NT, which went two down.

At the other table West, playing Precision, opened one diamond.

East responded 1NT, showing fair values in the system, and South came in with two diamonds, indicating length in both majors. Now what is the sense in that? I cannot see any point in distributional overcalls when it is clear beyond any doubt that the opponents have the balance of the cards. It is better to let them bid in the dark, as it were, and then be defeated by bad distribution.

On this occasion East-West bid to four clubs, which was doubled by North and would certainly have been defeated; but South, understandably nervous, retreated to four spades and lost 300.

In general, 4-4-4-1 is bad for attack; the lack of a side suit is a distinct disadvantage when you have no length in the trump suit. 5-3-3-2 is, at best, innocuous; it is always wrong to press for game when you hold this distribution. 5-4-3-1, on the other hand, almost always plays well. And there is quite a difference between 6-3-2-2 (often disappointing) and 6-3-3-1. Players who count points and don't take note of distribution are a menace.

46

Neither Puff Nor Blow

There is a standard question – What would you bid? Almost equally important is – *How* would you bid (or pass)? This little story will show you what I mean.

Neither side is vulnerable and in fourth position you hold:

♠ A 10 8 3
♡ A Q J 9 3
◇ —
♣ J 10 3 2

The bidding goes:

South	West	North	East
1♡	2◇	No	?

What would you say now? In a women's international match East at one table bid 2NT, which looks reasonable enough. Her partner went back to three diamonds and all passed. This was one down, the full hand being:

♠ J 9 7 6 2
♡ 6
◇ Q 7 4
♣ Q 7 6 5

♠ K 4
♡ 7
◇ K 10 8 6 5 3 2
♣ A 8 4

♠ A 10 8 3
♡ A Q J 9 3
◇ —
♣ J 10 3 2

♠ Q 5
♡ K 10 8 5 4 2
◇ A J 9
♣ K 9

At the other table the redoubtable partnership of Rixi Markus and Fritzi Gordon was East–West. This time the bidding went:

South	West	North	East
	Rixi		Fritzi
1♡	2◇	No	No
2♡	No	No	Dble
No	No	No	

Rixi found the dynamic lead of the king of spades and the declarer, who did not, perhaps, make the most of her opportunities, finished four down, conceding 700.

The point about this deal is not so much that Fritzi passed over her partner's two diamonds but that she passed 'in tempo'. That's where the difference lies between one top player and another. If East gives just that extra moment of consideration before saying 'No bid' (or, if bidding boxes are in use, before placing her card on the table), South is warned that the balance of strength lies with the enemy.

47

Not by Design

'My partner and I bid and made six hearts on this deal,' wrote a correspondent. 'Somebody pointed out afterwards that a grand slam could have been made in clubs. How would an expert pair have bid the hand to arrive at a contract of seven clubs?'

The question contains an assumption that is far from accurate, either in theory or practice. I doubt whether any pair would end up by design in seven clubs, but the deal is nevertheless instructive.

Dealer South   Game all

♠ 9
♡ K Q J 7 2
◇ A J 10 8 4
♣ A 5

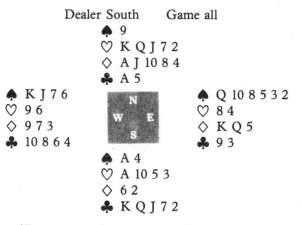

♠ K J 7 6   ♠ Q 10 8 5 3 2
♡ 9 6   ♡ 8 4
◇ 9 7 3   ◇ K Q 5
♣ 10 8 6 4   ♣ 9 3

♠ A 4
♡ A 10 5 3
◇ 6 2
♣ K Q J 7 2

South will open one club, North will respond in hearts, and South will raise. Players very seldom abandon the major suit after this beginning, except occasionally to play in notrumps. Still, neither player should close his mind to the possibility of finding a better suit contract. Say that the bidding proceeds on these lines:

South	West	North	East
1♣	No	2♡	No
3♡	No	4◇	No
4♠	No	5♣	No
6♣	No	?	

After the hearts have been raised, both players show controls and the natural interpretation of South's six clubs is that it shows a good suit. Now it is by no means impossible for North to work out that there are five top tricks in hearts, five in clubs, two aces and, *playing in clubs*, a thirteenth trick from the ruff in spades.

The reason why the hand plays better in clubs, which are 5–2, than in hearts, which are 5–4, is that the long clubs will not provide enough discards to avert a diamond loser. Looking at it another way, the extra trick, on this as on most occasions, will come from a ruff in the hand that has the shorter trumps.

Players are accustomed to the idea that to play in a trump suit divided 4–4 or 5–4 is always right; but as this hand shows, there is no advantage unless a side suit can be ruffed in the hand that has the shorter trumps.

48

Anything Funny About the Bidding?

How do you make a grand slam at notrumps when an opponent has the ace of clubs on the table – face down and ready to cash? It happened in the third qualifying round of the world championship at Biarritz.

Dealer South   E-W vulnerable

```
                    ♠ A K Q 9 8
                    ♡ A K Q 7
                    ◇ J 9 7
                    ♣ 8
♠ 10 6 5 4 2                         ♠ J 7 3
♡ 9 8 5            N                 ♡ 6 4 3
◇ —             W     E              ◇ 5 4 2
♣ K 7 6 5 2        S                 ♣ A 10 9 3
                    ♠ —
                    ♡ J 10 2
                    ◇ A K Q 10 8 6 3
                    ♣ Q J 4
```

This was the bidding:

South	West	North	East
1◇	No	1♠	No
2◇	No	2♡	No
3NT	No	5♣(1)	No
5♡(2)	No	6♣(3)	No
7◇(4)	No	No	Dble
No	No	No	

(1) Described as 'super Gerber', asking for aces; presumably four clubs would have had some other meaning in the system.

(2) One ace.

(3) A bit mysterious; I think he was giving partner a chance to bid 6NT if he held the king of clubs. In a pairs event this could make a big difference to the score.

(4) Not on the same wavelength.

After the final pass East placed a card (doubtless the ace of clubs) face down on the table, saying 'Is there anything funny about the bidding?'

South replied: 'Well, the first funny thing is that it's not your lead.'

West now had to find the club lead that would defeat the contract. Perhaps he thought to himself, 'I must not take note of East's misunderstanding. Technically, his double would suggest a spade lead.' At any rate, West led a spade and North–South scored a top, about 378 match points instead of a zero. Which was better than they deserved, for sensible players would bid the hand in a few seconds:

South	North
1♢	2♠
4♢	6♢
No	

South's jump rebid, after the force, indicates in Acol a solid suit with no other top control.

49

They May Turn and Bite

When opponents drop the bidding at a low level it is often right to reopen on moderate values. Indeed, I have seen it stated in print that it is always right to contest when opponents stop bidding at the two level. That goes too far. It is wise to distinguish between these two sequences:

	South	*West*	*North*	*East*
(1)	—	1 ◇	No	1 ♡
	No	2 ◇	No	No
	?			

	South	*West*	*North*	*East*
(2)	—	1 ◇	No	1 ♡
	No	2 ♡	No	No
	?			

In the first sequence the opponents have not found a fit and East may have a fair 4–4–1–4 type, on which he will be quick to turn and bite if South reopens.

In the second example East–West have found at least a mild fit in a major suit and have still subsided at the two level. They are more limited now; also, since they have a fit in hearts there is a built-in presumption that your side will have a fit somewhere. Thus on all grounds it is safer to contest after the second sequence than after the first.

[108]

South took an unjustified risk on this deal from a pairs event:

Dealer West   N-S vulnerable

```
                    ♠ J 10 5
                    ♡ 10 9 6
                    ◇ 9 6 5 4 3
                    ♣ A 4
   ♠ A K 6 4                        ♠ 7 3 2
   ♡ A Q 5 2          N             ♡ 8 4 3
   ◇ 7            W       E         ◇ A J 10 8 2
   ♣ Q 9 8 3          S             ♣ K 5
                    ♠ Q 9 8
                    ♡ K J 7
                    ◇ K Q
                    ♣ J 10 7 6 2
```

This was the bidding:

South	West	North	East
—	1♣	No	1◇
No	1♠	No	No
1NT	No	No	Dble
No	No	No	

South assumed too readily that the cards were equally divided between the two sides. He won the first heart and played ace and another club. East led a heart to the queen and West switched to a low spade. When he came in with the queen of clubs he cashed three spades and two hearts. South, down to ◇ K Q and ♣ 10, was squeezed. His venture had cost him 1100.

50

Careless Talk

Do light overcalls pay? This is one of the most debated questions among tournament players. Some say, 'Take no notice of my non-vulnerable overcalls at the one level.' Others prefer to maintain the traditional standards, though paying some attention to the space principle – that is to say, to the idea that a weak overcall should at least deprive the opponents of bidding space.

My own view of this matter is that the development of negative doubles has much reduced the occasional advantage of weak overcalls. Players are now better able to cope with them, and the disadvantages remain: loss of accuracy, and the giving away of information that is more likely to assist opponents than obstruct them. Quite often the weak overcall helps opponents to arrive at a more or less unbiddable game or slam.

Dealer South   N–S vulnerable

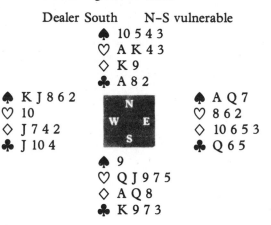

```
                    ♠ 10 5 4 3
                    ♡ A K 4 3
                    ◇ K 9
                    ♣ A 8 2
♠ K J 8 6 2                          ♠ A Q 7
♡ 10                                 ♡ 8 6 2
◇ J 7 4 2                            ◇ 10 6 5 3
♣ J 10 4                             ♣ Q 6 5
                    ♠ 9
                    ♡ Q J 9 7 5
                    ◇ A Q 8
                    ♣ K 9 7 3
```

South, in match play, opened one heart at both tables. At the first table West passed. North bid four clubs, a conventional way to indicate a fairly strong raise to game. South could bid only four hearts, and there they rested.

At the other table, where the American internationals, Weichsel and Sontag, were North–South, the bidding went like this:

South	West	North	East
1♡	1♠(1)	Dble	2♠
Dble(2)	No	6♡(3)	No
No	No		

(1) Especially foolish, because he is not depriving the opponents of bidding space (as would one spade over one club).

(2) Also a negative double. His hand is improved when it appears that both opponents have values in spades.

(3) North knows that his partner has a singleton spade at most, so he makes the value bid.

There was no problem in the play. If spades are led and continued, South may play on reverse dummy lines. Alternatively, as the cards lie, he can discard a club from dummy on the third round of diamonds and ruff a club.

51

Follow Your Instinct

There are times when you may feel that no-one could blame you for following course A, but that course B is more likely to win the money. Most players nervously think, 'Partner wants me to do such-and-such, I'm sure it's wrong but I'm not going to take the blame.'

<pre>
              Dealer North   N–S vulnerable
                        ♠ A Q
                        ♡ A 9 6 3
                        ◇ K J 4
                        ♣ K J 9 5
        ♠ 10 8 5 3   N   ♠ 9 4
        ♡ 7   W   E   ♡ J 8
        ◇ 10 8 6 5 3   ◇ A Q 2
        ♣ 7 6 4   S   ♣ A Q 10 8 3 2
                        ♠ K J 7 6 2
                        ♡ K Q 10 5 4 2
                        ◇ 9 7
                        ♣ —
</pre>

The bidding went:

South	West	North	East
—	—	1♣	No
1♠ (1)	No	2NT	No
4♡	No	6♡	Dble (2)
Redble (3)	No	No	No

(1) It is quite common, with 5–6 in the majors and not enough strength for a reverse, to open one spade; but when responding

there seems little point in bidding the shorter suit first.

(2) Since a diamond lead is quite likely on the bidding, it seems silly to ask for a club.

(3) Also not well judged. South may have thought: 'He's asking for a club lead, but that won't do much good, I'll teach him a lesson.'

Now West was in the situation described above: 'South must know that East is asking for a club lead,' he said to himself, 'and I dare say a diamond would be best, but nobody can blame me if I lead a club.'

This was not much consolation when South ruffed the club lead, drew trumps, and discarded three diamonds from dummy on the long spades. Some painful calculation revealed that, counting 700 for the rubber, this was worth 2620 to North–South instead of minus 400.

'I would have led a diamond if you hadn't doubled,' said West, getting his blow in first.

'But you heard the redouble,' East replied. 'Why didn't you change your mind?'

'I thought he was bluffing, to put me off the club lead' was West's improbable excuse.

Part IV – Famous Hands
Deals 52 – 65

52

A Half in Six

On most occasions you would be quite pleased to pick up this hand:

♠ —
♡ A 3
◇ A K 10 8 3
♣ A K Q 5 4 2

But the attractions diminish when there are two bids in front of you – one spade on your left and three hearts on your right. You are told that the jump to three hearts is pre-emptive. It's the last board of a critical match. What would you say now?

Dealer West   E–W vulnerable

        ♠ K J 10 7 5 3 2
        ♡ 10 8
        ◇ 9 4 2
        ♣ 7

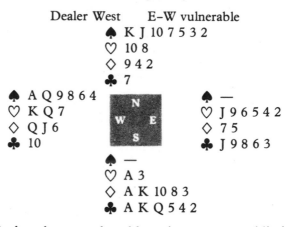

♠ A Q 9 8 6 4   ♠ —
♡ K Q 7   ♡ J 9 6 5 4 2
◇ Q J 6   ◇ 7 5
♣ 10   ♣ J 9 8 6 3

        ♠ —
        ♡ A 3
        ◇ A K 10 8 3
        ♣ A K Q 5 4 2

East's three hearts, vulnerable against not, seems idiotic to me, but some Americans – this was the Spingold Trophy – follow this style.

South in practice bid 5NT, forcing his partner to six diamonds. Against the bad distribution North had to play well to go only one down.

The bidding at the other table was also unusual:

South	West	North	East
—	1♠	No	No
2♠	Dble	No	No
4♠	No	No	No

South's four spades was a loud cry for a minor suit, but his partner took the view (quite wrongly, I feel) that game in spades would be easier than in any other denomination.

So South became declarer in four spades – a fate he can hardly have anticipated when he picked up his cards. West led the king of hearts and after winning with the ace South led ace and king of clubs. West ruffed and North overruffed. Then declarer came back to hand with a diamond and led another high club. In the end West made only four tricks, which no doubt was less than he expected in view of his trump holding.

So the board was tied, after what golfers might describe as an adventurous half in six.

53

The Wind on His Face

Suppose that in the South position you pick up:

> ♠ A K Q 9 5
> ♡ Q 7 2
> ◇ A K 9 6
> ♣ 4

At love all your partner, North, opens 3NT – standard procedure with a solid minor and not much else. The next player passes. What do you respond?

Playing in the (American) Summer Nationals about 37 years ago, William Hanna ventured 6NT. No doubt he realized that there were at least two losing hearts, but there was no reason to assume that a heart would be led. However, the bidding was not over. When 6NT came round to East, he doubled. What now? This, in fact, was the full hand:

Dealer North   Love all

```
                    ♠ 10 4
                    ♡ J 6 3
                    ◇ 4
                    ♣ A K Q J 6 5 2
  ♠ 8 7 6 3 2                         ♠ J
  ♡ 8 4            N                  ♡ A K 10 9 5
  ◇ Q 10 8 5 3   W   E                ◇ J 7 2
  ♣ 7              S                  ♣ 10 9 8 3
                    ♠ A K Q 9 5
                    ♡ Q 7 2
                    ◇ A K 9 6
                    ♣ 4
```

The bidding so far, you will recall, has been:

South	West	North	East
—	—	3NT	No
6NT	No	No	Dble
?			

South, who could feel the wind on his face, transferred to seven clubs, on his singleton. East simply had to double again. And you can guess the end of the story: West led a spade, not a heart.

When West had finished his grumble about East's double of 6NT, East pointed out, with some justification, that a short suit lead of a heart would have been more sensible on West's hand. 'We get them two down,' he added.

Hanna's transfer to seven clubs was widely praised, but don't you think he should have bid six clubs on the first round if he was going to gamble? The point is that East, leading through the strong hand (in 6NT) might well lead an ace or low from a king. But West, with the same sort of holding in hearts, might hesitate to lead this suit.

54

The Finesse That Never Was

Some hands are a little puzzling in that the contract appears to be lay-down but the match records proclaim failure. Consider this deal from a match between Canada and Mexico. The Canadians played in the obvious contract of four hearts and West led his singleton club. The defenders are entitled to a spade, a diamond, and a club ruff if the trumps are not drawn at once, but that is all, since the ruff consumes the trump trick; or so it would seem.

Dealer East   Love all

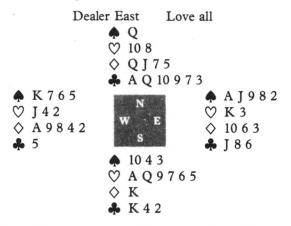

♠ Q
♡ 10 8
◇ Q J 7 5
♣ A Q 10 9 7 3

♠ K 7 6 5
♡ J 4 2
◇ A 9 8 4 2
♣ 5

♠ A J 9 8 2
♡ K 3
◇ 10 6 3
♣ J 8 6

♠ 10 4 3
♡ A Q 9 7 6 5
◇ K
♣ K 4 2

The Canadians were playing five-card majors, with a response of 1NT forcing for one round (as in Precision). So the bidding went: one heart – 1NT, two hearts – four hearts (since South was marked was a six-card suit).

West led his singleton club, won in dummy. Declarer cannot risk a heart finesse at once. He played a diamond to the king and ace; then came a spade to the ace and a club ruff, leaving:

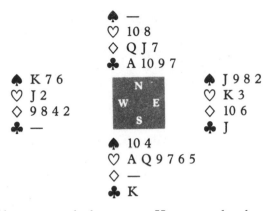

```
              ♠ —
              ♡ 10 8
              ◇ Q J 7
              ♣ A 10 9 7
♠ K 7 6                        ♠ J 9 8 2
♡ J 2         N                ♡ K 3
◇ 9 8 4 2   W   E              ◇ 10 6
♣ —           S                ♣ J
              ♠ 10 4
              ♡ A Q 9 7 6 5
              ◇ —
              ♣ K
```

South appears to be home now. However, when he won the next diamond in dummy and played the ten of hearts to the queen, West dropped the jack. Thinking that East still held K x in hearts, South tried to enter dummy with a club, intending to cash one more diamond, then finesse in trumps. Unlucky! West was there first with the concealed two of hearts.

It was a simple trick by the Mexican defender, Reygadas, but for some reason the play of dropping the jack is seldom seen, though obviously it cannot cost.

55

Not To Be Repeated

Not many people could tell you much about the 1963 Par Point Olympiad, as it was called. The 32 deals were composed by two Australians, who must have constructed them with wet towels round their heads, because many were exceedingly difficult. The event was not repeated. Even with all the cards exposed, you will not easily see the point of this deal:

```
              Dealer North      Love all
                     ♠ 6 5 4 2
                     ♡ K 4
                     ◇ A 9 7 3
                     ♣ 7 4 2
   ♠ 3                              ♠ 10 9 8 7
   ♡ J 5 2           N              ♡ Q 9 6
   ◇ K 10 5 4     W     E           ◇ J 8 6
   ♣ A K 9 6 5       S              ♣ J 8 3
                     ♠ A K Q J
                     ♡ A 10 8 7 3
                     ◇ Q 2
                     ♣ Q 10
```

To earn full points for bidding, North–South had to stay short of game, which seems a little harsh; but the so-called Directed Contract was four spades by South.

West leads the king of clubs and East, not wishing to suggest a switch to any other suit, may play the 8. In any case, on the second round East must drop the *jack*. Otherwise, when the jack is played on the third trick South (following instructions) will discard a diamond and East will be on lead with no effective play.

There is more to it. When West, after his partner's play of the jack, follows with the nine of clubs South (following the same instruction) discards the two of diamonds. Then West leads a fourth club, East discards a heart and the position is:

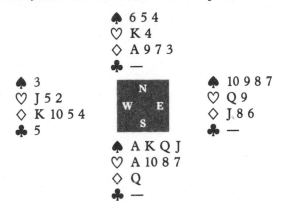

```
              ♠ 6 5 4
              ♡ K 4
              ◇ A 9 7 3
              ♣ —
♠ 3                           ♠ 10 9 8 7
♡ J 5 2          N            ♡ Q 9
◇ K 10 5 4    W     E         ◇ J 8 6
♣ 5              S            ♣ —
              ♠ A K Q J
              ♡ A 10 8 7
              ◇ Q
              ♣ —
```

Now when South, who has already lost three tricks, tries to ruff the third round of hearts, he is overruffed. The hand is fair, I suppose, and a better test than many in the event, but the defenders, as you will have seen, need to find a series of very good plays.

56

Moderate Marking

This was another difficult deal in the 1963 Par Point Olympiad, set by two Australians, M.J. Sullivan and R.E. Williams:

```
          Dealer South      Love all
                ♠ 2
                ♡ Q 6 5 4 3 2
                ◇ A 5 3 2
                ♣ 4 2
♠ K Q 10 9 8 7 6 5 4 3           ♠ J
♡ K 7                            ♡ 10 9 8
◇ Q                             ◇ J 10 9 8
♣ —                             ♣ 10 8 7 6 5
                ♠ A
                ♡ A J
                ◇ K 7 6 4
                ♣ A K Q J 9 3
```

Once again, the award for bidding was hardly fair. South, one assumes, will open two clubs, and West will overcall with four spades. If South at his turn bids five clubs, it is reasonable for North to bid six clubs. This would have cost points, but the Directed Contract, nevertheless, was indeed six clubs.

West leads a spade and the fall of the jack tells South (since in general false-carding was not allowed) that East has a singleton. On the first round of clubs West shows out. It is natural now for South to lead the six of diamonds to dummy, pick up the trumps, and hope to re-enter dummy on the fourth round of diamonds for a heart finesse.

This is the wrong plan, however. It costs nothing to begin with the king of diamonds, on which West's queen falls. With a count of West's hand, South exits with ace and jack of hearts, which leaves:

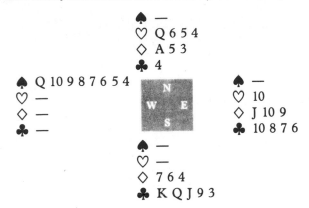

```
                    ♠ —
                    ♡ Q 6 5 4
                    ◇ A 5 3
                    ♣ 4
 ♠ Q 10 9 8 7 6 5 4                      ♠ —
 ♡ —                                     ♡ 10
 ◇ —                                     ◇ J 10 9
 ♣ —                                     ♣ 10 8 7 6
                    ♠ —
                    ♡ —
                    ◇ 7 6 4
                    ♣ K Q J 9 3
```

West has to lead a spade, dummy ruffs with the 4 of clubs, and South underruffs with the 3. Then winning hearts are led from the table and East is caught in a trump coup.

If anyone played it this way, he certainly deserved his points. Claude Rodrigue and I, who had won the previous event of this kind in 1961, could muster only 124 out of 200, but this was still the best score I heard of on our cards. Tony Priday and Jeremy Flint scored 129, playing in the other direction.

57

Underground Journey

In 1957 a par contest and also a pairs tournament were played at Selfridges to celebrate the 150th anniversary of De La Rue, one of whose enterprises was the manufacture of playing cards. Harold Franklin and I were entrusted to prepare the 16 deals for the par contest. As the competitors were all experts, drawn from about fifteen countries, we naturally set out to produce a difficult set. This one was a test for the defending side:

Dealer South   N–S vulnerable

```
              ♠ J 7 2
              ♡ Q 8 6 5
              ◇ A Q J
              ♣ K 5 2
   ♠ 4                        ♠ A 8 6
   ♡ J 10 9 7 3 2     N       ♡ A
   ◇ 7 6            W   E      ◇ 9 8 5 3 2
   ♣ J 8 6 3           S      ♣ A Q 7 4
              ♠ K Q 10 9 5 3
              ♡ K 4
              ◇ K 10 4
              ♣ 10 9
```

North–South scored maximum points for bidding to four spades, with consolation for three spades. West leads the jack of hearts and East wins with the ace. This was the analysis of the play:

'East wins the first trick with the ace of hearts and can see promise of three defensive tricks – but will he live to enjoy the queen of clubs as well? South is sure to have five tricks in spades, two in hearts, and three in diamonds, if given time to make them.

'There is only one chance – that West holds the jack of clubs. At trick two East returns the queen of clubs, tunnelling a way into his partner's hand. Winning the first or second round of spades, East plays a low club to his partner's jack and the contest ends happily for him (it was board 16) when he ruffs a heart to defeat the contract.'

I happened to be watching when the famous Charles Goren defended this hand. He found the club return at trick two all right, but unlucky! He chose a low club instead of the queen, and this, of course, killed the entry to this partner's hand.

Harold and I were pleased, I remember, that although many of the plays were tricky, all were accomplished by at least one pair. The best score was returned by Norman Squire and Albert Rose, 77 out of 100 as North–South. Second equal were Bourchtoff and Svarc, of France, MacLaren and Forbes, of Scotland, with 73 as East–West.

58

Wait for It!

One hand in the 1957 par contest doesn't look too difficult but was correctly managed at only one table.

Dealer North   N–S vulnerable

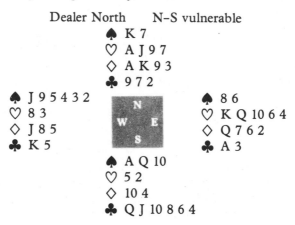

```
                 ♠ K 7
                 ♡ A J 9 7
                 ♢ A K 9 3
                 ♣ 9 7 2
 ♠ J 9 5 4 3 2                    ♠ 8 6
 ♡ 8 3                            ♡ K Q 10 6 4
 ♢ J 8 5                          ♢ Q 7 6 2
 ♣ K 5                            ♣ A 3
                 ♠ A Q 10
                 ♡ 5 2
                 ♢ 10 4
                 ♣ Q J 10 8 6 4
```

North might open 1NT, but the suggested bidding was:

South	West	North	East
—	—	1♡	No
2♣	No	2♢	No
2NT	No	3NT	Dble
No	No	No	

North–South scored their points for reaching 3NT and there was no bidding par for East-West.

West, in response to his partner's lead-directing double, begins with the eight of hearts, which is covered by the nine and ten. East then . . .

Oh dear, did you miss it too? East must *not* part with the ten of hearts: he must leave his partner with a heart to lead when he comes in with a club honour. It's like those situations when you hold A Q J x x over dummy's K x and partner has led from a doubleton.

Quite a few players, on the other hand, found the answer to this deal:

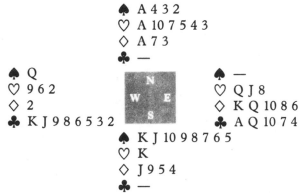

♠ A 4 3 2
♡ A 10 7 5 4 3
◇ A 7 3
♣ —

♠ Q
♡ 9 6 2
◇ 2
♣ K J 9 8 6 5 3 2

♠ —
♡ Q J 8
◇ K Q 10 8 6
♣ A Q 10 7 4

♠ K J 10 9 8 7 6 5
♡ K
◇ J 9 5 4
♣ —

South plays in six spades after East has opened one diamond. Declarer wins the diamond lead in dummy and sees that, because of the awkward block in spades, a heart to the king, spade to the ace, then ace and another heart, won't help him. Instead, he must let West's queen of spades hold the third trick!

The commentary ended on an ironic note: 'Tricky, but if we had wanted to make the hand difficult we would have given West the singleton six of spades instead of the queen.'

59

A Noble Sacrifice

The pairs tournament that was run alongside the par contest at Selfridges in 1957 (see preceding pages) was won by Charles Goren and Helen Sobel. Helen had a great reputation in America and the British audience had a chance to estimate her talent on the following deal from the par contest:

Dealer South   Game all

```
                      ♠ A Q 7
                      ♡ 5 4 3
                      ◇ 6 5 3 2
                      ♣ 9 7 2
  ♠ K J 10 9 8 6 4 2           ♠ 5 3
  ♡ 10 9                       ♡ Q J 8 7 2
  ◇ K 4                        ◇ —
  ♣ Q                          ♣ J 8 6 5 4 3
                      ♠ —
                      ♡ A K 6
                      ◇ A Q J 10 9 8 7
                      ♣ A K 10
```

The suggested bidding (on which the play should be based) was:

South	West	North	East
2♣	3♠	3NT	No
6◇	No	No	No

The bidding par was generous, North–South scoring the maximum for six diamonds or for a game bid in diamonds or notrumps or a double of five spades or higher.

Each pair in turn came into the 'Fish Bowl' and I did a commentary on the play with the aid of a sort of Vu-Graph. Helen Sobel was West and I gave the deal a big build-up – great test for a great player sort of thing.

My oration fell a little flat, because when West made the directed lead of the ten of hearts and South won, then led the ace of diamonds, Helen dropped the king as though it were the card nearest her thumb. You see the point? West can gauge that if she keeps the king of diamonds South will cash heart and club winners, then exit with a diamond, forcing a lead into dummy's A Q of spades.

There was a further point in the deal. After the king of diamonds has fallen under the ace, South will draw trumps and cash the king of hearts and the ace of clubs, on which West's queen falls. It is not too difficult then for declarer to organize an end-play against East, who at the finish is thrown in with a heart and forced to lead into ♣ K 10.

However the hand ended, West scored full points for the defence for dropping the king of diamonds under the ace, and South scored his par for making twelve tricks, whatever the defence.

60

Military Wisdom

'Defend me from my friends; I can defend myself from my enemies.' So cried a French general to Louis XIV long before bridge was invented. After trying to defeat 3NT on this deal, East knew exactly what the general meant.

Dealer South   E–W vulnerable

```
                    ♠ Q 7 6 4
                    ♡ J 7 5
                    ◇ K 7 3
                    ♣ 9 6 2
   ♠ 8 5 2                          ♠ J 10
   ♡ K 9 3              N           ♡ 10 8 6 4
   ◇ 10 6 4 2      W         E      ◇ A 8 5
   ♣ Q J 4              S           ♣ K 10 8 7
                    ♠ A K 9 3
                    ♡ A Q 2
                    ◇ Q J 9
                    ♣ A 5 3
```

The hand occurred in a match between France and Switzerland. This was the bidding when the French were North–South:

South	West	North	East
2NT	No	3NT	No
No	No		

Note that North refrained from bidding an idiotic three clubs over 2NT; in four spades there are four certain losers.

West opened a low diamond against 3NT and the declarer put up the king from dummy. Now Pietro Bernasconi, in the East chair, made two swift deductions.

One was that the declarer must hold ◇ Q J and must be prepared for the defence to take the ace and continue diamonds. The second was that the diamonds would not produce enough tricks to beat the contract. The only suit where the defence might take three tricks was clubs, and if he took the ace of diamonds East would be giving up the entry for the thirteenth club.

Pietro, therefore, played low on the king of diamonds – in less time than it takes to tell. Now South finessed the queen of hearts. West won but, unhappily for the defence, did not find the switch to a club. Misreading the situation, he led another diamond, and then the declarer had nine tricks.

When I first wrote about this hand I remarked that declarer would have made the contract if he had read the diamond situation and knocked out the ace of diamonds instead of taking the heart finesse. Not so, a correspondent pointed out. East can win the second round of diamonds and switch to clubs; when South holds up for two rounds West reverts to diamonds and now makes the king of hearts and the thirteenth diamond.

61

Golden Oldie

The annals of bridge include many famous hands, and here is one of the strangest ever recorded. It was played between Austria and Germany in the European Championship at Montreux in 1954.

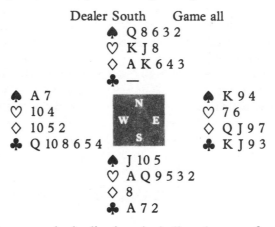

Dealer South   Game all

```
                    ♠ Q 8 6 3 2
                    ♡ K J 8
                    ◇ A K 6 4 3
                    ♣ —
    ♠ A 7                         ♠ K 9 4
    ♡ 10 4                        ♡ 7 6
    ◇ 10 5 2                      ◇ Q J 9 7
    ♣ Q 10 8 6 5 4               ♣ K J 9 3
                    ♠ J 10 5
                    ♡ A Q 9 5 3 2
                    ◇ 8
                    ♣ A 7 2
```

With so much duplication, including the ace of a short suit opposite a void, it is easy for North–South to climb too high. Indeed this happened at both tables. At the first table, where the legendary Austrian player, Karl Schneider, was the declarer, the final contract was six hearts.

West led a club and dummy ruffed. If it were not for entry problems South might plan to discard one spade on the king of diamonds and one on a fifth diamond, but this line cannot be combined with two club ruffs. Schneider saw this at once and at the second trick led a low spade to the jack and ace. West led a second club, ruffed in dummy, and the king of hearts was overtaken by the ace. When the trumps were led out West let go a diamond and on the last heart East was squeezed in spades and diamonds. The West player had not distinguished himself.

The German North at the other table, Egmont von Dewitz, played in six spades, which looks still more difficult. However, anything you can do I can do better, as the song goes.

East led a club, taken by the ace. Declarer led the jack of spades from South (the dummy), and all played low. North shrewdly crossed to the ace of diamonds and led the next spade from hand.

'Is he trying to catch me?' East wondered. 'Did I hesitate on the first round of trumps?' After agonized thought East put up the king, crashing his partner's ace.

Go back for a moment to the contract of six hearts. There is another way in which this might be made – at any rate, if South has not supported the spades. As before, declarer wins the heart lead in dummy and plays a spade to the jack and ace. West exits with a second trump. Now a low spade from the table would give East an anxious moment. To play the king might be wrong if South had begun with a singleton jack.

62

Goodnight Vienna

In a European Championship match at Lausanne, where I was doing the Vu-Graph commentary, the Yugoslav player, Dragoslav Velovic, had an unfortunate experience when playing against Italy.

Dealer South   N–S vulnerable

```
              ♠ 6
              ♡ A 7 5 2
              ◇ A 10 3
              ♣ K J 10 6 4
♠ K J 10 2                      ♠ 9 7 5 4 3
♡ 6 4                           ♡ 9
◇ K 5 4                         ◇ Q J 9 8 6
♣ Q 8 3 2                       ♣ 7 5
              ♠ A Q 8
              ♡ K Q J 10 8 3
              ◇ 7 2
              ♣ A 9
```

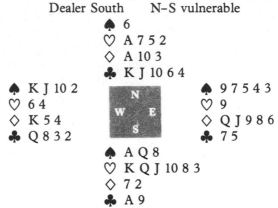

The bidding, as reported, is a little mystifying:

South	West	North	East
1♡	No	2♣	No
3◇	No	3♡	No
6♡	No	7♡	No
No	No		

Whatever the significance of the early bids, the Yugoslavs evidently knew what they were doing, for seven hearts is a splendid contract. The obvious plan, after a trump lead, is to set up a fifth club, using spade ruffs for entry to the dummy.

The declarer began correctly by drawing a second trump. Then he pulled out the ace of spades, put it back, and played on clubs, ruffing the third round. It was time now for ace of spades and a spade ruff, to be followed by another club ruff. But alas! Confused by his earlier hesitancy, or perhaps excited to have bid a good grand slam against such celebrated opposition, Velovic led the eight of spades, forgetting that he had not laid down the ace.

The Italians were sympathetic, of course, but nevertheless wrote down +100 on the scoresheet.

Velovic's partner, according to the onlookers, got up from his chair and came round the table to embrace him. Can you think of one or two partners who might have acted differently?

The blow was partially mitigated by the fact that the Italians at the other table played in 6NT and went down after a diamond lead. I wonder how the play went. South will duck the first trick. Suppose that East wins and returns a spade. The best play now is to cross to the ace of diamonds – a funny sort of Vienna coup – then run the hearts. West, with the king of spades and the long clubs, will be in dire trouble. Note that the timing for the squeeze is wrong if the ace of diamonds is not cashed.

63

Out for the Count

This is another deal from the European Championship at Lausanne in 1979. The Swedish team, which had won in Denmark the previous year, was fancied to win again, but their form was inconsistent and they finished in the middle. Here the Swedish declarer showed a costly lack of concentration; I will give you a chance to do better.

♠ 7 3 2
♡ K J 8 4 3
♢ A 5 4
♣ 7 3

♣ Q led

♠ A K Q J 10 4
♡ A 10 9 2
♢ K 9
♣ 10

Your side is vulnerable and the bidding has been:

South	West	North	East
—	No	No	5♣
Dble	No	5♡	No
6♠	No	No	No

The queen of clubs is overtaken and East leads a second round.

You ruff high and West discards a diamond. East shows out on the first spade, so you have to draw four rounds. All follow to two rounds of diamonds. You continue with ace and ten of hearts, West playing low. Do you play for the drop or do you finesse?

Well, you can't be sure; but if you had played a third round of diamonds East would have shown out and you would have had a perfect count. The full hand was:

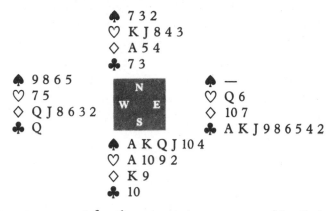

```
                    ♠ 7 3 2
                    ♡ K J 8 4 3
                    ◇ A 5 4
                    ♣ 7 3
  ♠ 9 8 6 5                        ♠ —
  ♡ 7 5            N               ♡ Q 6
  ◇ Q J 8 6 3 2  W   E             ◇ 10 7
  ♣ Q              S               ♣ A K J 9 8 6 5 4 2
                    ♠ A K Q J 10 4
                    ♡ A 10 9 2
                    ◇ K 9
                    ♣ 10
```

When you are out for the count you must assemble all the evidence you can. Playing three rounds of diamonds would have taken your last trump, but no matter. It was an extraordinary mistake for a good player not to play a third diamond to discover the heart situation. As Mohammed Ali would have said, 'The queen falls in two.'

[139]

64

Walter Sees Round Corners

Some bridge hands have the kind of elegance that is admired in famous games of chess. This deal was played in a world championship match between Italy and the United States.

Dealer South   E–W vulnerable

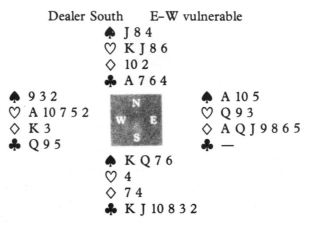

```
                   ♠ J 8 4
                   ♡ K J 8 6
                   ◇ 10 2
                   ♣ A 7 6 4
  ♠ 9 3 2                         ♠ A 10 5
  ♡ A 10 7 5 2                    ♡ Q 9 3
  ◇ K 3                           ◇ A Q J 9 8 6 5
  ♣ Q 9 5                         ♣ —
                   ♠ K Q 7 6
                   ♡ 4
                   ◇ 7 4
                   ♣ K J 10 8 3 2
```

This was the bidding when Italy was East-West:

South	West	North	East
No	No	No	1◇
2♣	2♡	3♣	4♡
4♠	Dble	5♣	No
No	Dble	No	No
No			

Assuming that he takes the right view in clubs, it looks as though South will lose just four tricks, does it not? Yet there is a defence to put him three down, and the Italians nearly found it.

Belladonna led the king of diamonds. Avarelli overtook with the ace, cashed the queen, and then led a surprising card, the nine of hearts. Belladonna returned a heart and there was still the ace of spades to come, for two down.

On this (rare) occasion Belladonna missed the significance of his partner's play. Look again at the position when he was in with the ace of hearts:

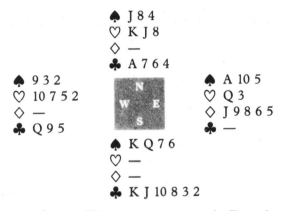

♠ J 8 4
♡ K J 8
◇ —
♣ A 7 6 4

♠ 9 3 2
♡ 10 7 5 2
◇ —
♣ Q 9 5

♠ A 10 5
♡ Q 3
◇ J 9 8 6 5
♣ —

♠ K Q 7 6
♡ —
◇ —
♣ K J 10 8 3 2

After ace of hearts West must return a spade. East wins and plays a third diamond, promoting a trump trick for West. (If South ruffs with the jack West declines to overruff). It was essential for the defence to cash the heart trick before making this play, because otherwise the declarer will discard his singleton heart on the third round of diamonds.

It was brilliant of Avarelli to visualize this position although he did not know the precise lie of the trumps.

65

Floodlights

At the big European tournaments prizes are awarded for the best dummy play and the best defence. The play that won the prize for defence at Wiesbaden in 1983 was the following:

Dealer West   E–W vulnerable

♠ K 10 8 4 3
♡ 8 6
◇ 9 6 4
♣ A K 6

♠ Q 9 2   ♠ 7 6
♡ 9 5 4   ♡ J 7 2
◇ A Q 5 2   ◇ J 10 8 7 3
♣ J 9 2   ♣ 10 7 4

♠ A J 5
♡ A K Q 10 3
◇ K
♣ Q 8 5 3

Somehow South, in the match between Iceland and Roumania, became the declarer in six spades. Perhaps South, playing in the style where the shorter suit is bid first on good hands, opened one spade; or perhaps he opened one heart and bid spades after a Drury two clubs (showing a strong pass) by his partner.

At any rate, the Icelandic West held the first trick with the ace of diamonds. What do you think he played next?

He made what seems a remarkable choice – the nine of spades, which ran to the declarer's jack. Sitting South, how would you assess the position? Perhaps the nine of spades was a singleton? In any case, it looks as though East holds the queen. So the declarer crossed to dummy with a club and ran the eight of spades. Unlucky, one down!

If you consider the situation you will see that this type of play might gain in several ways. For example:

(1)   (2)

          K 10 8 5 2   A J 9 7 4

Q 9 4   J   Q 5   8 6 2

      A 7 6 3   K 10 3

On (1) the lead of the nine is covered by the ten, jack and ace. Now South will surely play for the drop of the queen. Left to himself, he would cash the ace and probably finesse the ten on the next round, following the principle of restricted choice (meaning that if East had held Q J he might have played the queen on the first round).

On (2) the lead of the five is won by dummy's nine. On the next round South may well play low to the ten. Left to himself, he would normally begin with the king from hand.

One day you may bring off an unknown variant of this play and see your name in lights!